THE LIBRARY

CO CEA 772

ND
36

Suicide and the Older Adult

Edited by
Antoon A. Leenaars, PhD, CPsych
Ronald Maris, PhD
John L. McIntosh, PhD
Joseph Richman, PhD

The Guilford Press
New York   London

Published by The Guilford Press
A Division of Guilford Publications
72 Spring Street, New York, NY 10012

All rights reserved
No part of this book may be reproduced, stored in a
retrieval system, or transmitted, in any form or by any means,
electronic, mechanical, photocopying, microfilming,
recording, or otherwise, without permission in writing
from the Publisher.

© 1992 The American Association of Suicidology
Published simultaneously as *Suicide and Life-Threatening
Behavior*, Volume 22, Number 1, Spring 1992.

ISBN 0-89862-587-4

Last digit is print number: 9 8 7 6 5 4 3 2 1

Printed in the United States of America

SUICIDE AND THE OLDER ADULT

To our parents

Preface

Older adults have the highest rate of suicide in the United States and many other countries. Suicide in the elderly is often attributed to old age, terminal illness, or some other single characteristic. This is a myth. Suicide in the older adult is a multidimensional malaise. It is imperative that we understand this malaise. Yet, studies of suicide regarding older adults are scarce. I suspect that this perpetuates the above and numerous other myths about aging, death, and suicide in older adults. For this reason, we developed the current volume.

There is an urgent need for research, especially for studies that have clinical utility. As a researcher–clinician, I cannot but emphasize this point. As an example, there seem to be virtually no studies on the biology of elderly suicide. This volume should be seen as a step in an area requiring much greater clinical observation and scientific study.

In this volume, we attempt to engage in a process of understanding suicide in the older adult. To do this, we have been fortunate to obtain the cooperation of a highly competent group of contributors. I was equally fortunate to have available the consultative skills of J. Richman and J. McIntosh and the administrative direction of R. Maris, editor of *SLTB*.

By way of background, the following introduces our contributors in order of the appearance in the text.

Robert Kastenbaum, PhD, is Professor of Communication at Arizona State University, Tempe, Arizona. He is a past president of the American Association of Suicidology (AAS), the author of *The Psychology of Death, Death, Society, & Human Experience*, and editor of *Omega, Journal of Death and Dying*.

John McIntosh, PhD, is Associate Professor of Psychology at Indiana University at South Bend and Research Associate at the Center for Gerontological Education, Research and Services, at the University of Notre Dame. He is secretary of the AAS and editor/author of *Suicide and its Aftermath* and *Suicide and the Elderly: An Annotated Bibliography and Review*.

David Lester, PhD, is Executive Director at Center for Study of Suicide, Blackwood, NJ. He is president of the International Association for Suicide Prevention (IASP) and a prominent researcher in the field of suicidology. Bijou Yang, PhD, is Assistant Professor of Economics at Drexel University.

A. Hind Rifai, MD, is Assistant Professor of Psychiatry & Medicine and Director, Geriatric Research Unit, at Western Psychiatric Institute and Clinic, University of Pittsburgh School of Medicine. Dr. Rifai is a prominent scholar in geriatric research. Charles F. Reynolds, MD, is Professor of Psychiatry and Neurology and Director, Sleep Evaluation Center, at Western Psychiatric Institute and Clinic, University of Pittsburgh School of Medicine. J. John Mann, MD, is Professor of Psychiatry and Director, Laboratories of Neuropharmacology, at Western Psychiatric Institute and Clinic, University of Pittsburgh School of Medicine.

Antoon A. Leenaars, PhD, C Psych, is currently in private practice in Windsor, Canada. He is president of the Canadian Association of Suicide Prevention (CASP), & Board Member of AAS, and the author/editor of *Suicide Notes, Life Span Perspectives of Suicide* and *Suicide Prevention in Schools*.

Silvia Sara Canetto, PhD, is Assistant Professor, Department of Psychology at Colorado State University. Dr. Canetto is a prominent scholar in gender, life-threatening behaviors, and aging—the author of numerous publications in these areas.

Nancy J. Osgood, PhD, is Associate Professor of Gerontology and Sociology at Virginia Commonwealth University Medical College. She is known for her work on elderly suicide and is author/editor of *Suicide in the Elderly: A Practitioner's Guide to Diagnosis and Mental Health Intervention*, *Suicide Among the Elderly in Long-Term Care Facilities*, and *Suicide and the Elderly: An Annotated Bibliography and Review*.

Norman L. Farberow, PhD, is currently in private practice in Los Angeles and formerly Co-Director of the Los Angeles Suicide Prevention Center. He is a past president of AAS and the author/editor of numerous books including *Clues to Suicide*, *The Cry for Help*, and *The Many Faces of Suicide*. Dolores Gallagher-Thompson, PhD, is at Division of Gerontology, Stanford University School of Medicine and at the Geriatric Research and Education Center (GRECC), VA Medical Center, Palo Alto. Michael Gilewski, PhD, is at the Department of Physical Medicine and Rehabilitation, Cedars-Sinai Medical Center, Los Angeles, and Larry Thompson, PhD, is at the Older Adult and Family Center, Stanford University School of Medicine and GRECC.

Derek Humphry is the founder and Executive Director of the National Hemlock Society, Eugene, Oregon. He is author of the books *Jean's Way*, *The Right to Die*, *Let Me Die Before I Wake*, and *Final Exit*. In August of 1991, *Final Exit* reached the top of the New York Times bestseller list for advice books.

Joseph Richman, PhD, is currently in private practice in New York and Professor Emeritus at Albert Einstein College of Medicine, New York. He is a prominent scholar in gerentological suicidology and the author of *Family Therapy for Suicidal People* and *Overcoming Elderly Suicide.*

Allan L. Berman, PhD, is currently in private practice in Washington, DC, and Director at the National Center for the Study and Prevention of Suicide, Washington School of Psychiatry. He is a past president of AAS, the author/editor of *Suicide Prevention: Case Consultations* and *Adolescent Suicide: Assessment and Intervention.*

Suicide in the older adult can be prevented. These people are trapped in a condition of unbearable pain that is treatable. If we understand the malaise, if we improve the situation, if we provide alternatives, many people will survive. The older adults' age itself attests to viability.

From a broader social view: Is our society willing to provide the humane needs for older people? Are we willing to provide the support that these people, even when terminally ill, need? I suspect that there are many sterling benefits for our society if we do. Wisdom from our older people—including knowledge applicable to the field of suicidology itself—can likely assist in not only saving lives but preventing world destruction.

Antoon A. Leenaars, PhD, C Psych
September, 1991

1

Death, Suicide and the Older Adult

Robert Kastenbaum, PhD
Arizona State University

ABSTRACT: Elderly people who are at high risk for suicide often have characteristics that are associated with reduced opportunity or inclination to communicate (e.g., male, living alone, residing in a low-income transient urban area, suffering from a depressive state). This paper attempts to provide converging perspectives on death and suicide from the standpoints of both the external observer and the elderly person. An interpretation of the statistical pattern is followed by a critique of current policy proposals for limiting society's response to the needs of vulnerable people on the basis of a "natural life span." Studies of elderly people themselves reveal a great diversity of attitudes toward death that is not well served by generalizations and stereotypes. However, it appears that stressful conditions of life arouse more anxiety among older people than does the prospect of death.

Does the older person have a special relationship with death? And is suicide somehow a different proposition for the older person than for society? Questions such as these are best approached from converging perspectives. Most observations about death and suicide in old age have been made from the perspective of the external observer. Often the external observer has been a younger person who has not yet experienced the losses and stresses that are frequently associated with a long life. Even if this observer is fortified with statistics and other factual information, his or her interpretation is subject to influence by assumptions such as:

1. "Old people really don't have that much to live for."
2. "I might want to do myself in if I found myself in this person's situation."
3. "Realistically, there's no way either to change the situation in a significant way, or to change the mind of this stubborn and rigid old person."

1

These assumptions tend to perpetuate themselves because they are seldom recognized as assumptions, and because they accord well with the predisposition to avoid intensive contact with people who remind us of those twin unpleasantries, aging and death. Although the error of misattributing one's own thoughts and motives to others can be made in any situation, it is likelier to occur when the clinician or researcher is remote from the experiential world of the person who is at risk for suicide. A 40-year-old counselor working with a youth, for example, might be able to call upon his or her own experiences of adolescent confusion and stress, but would have no such personal resource to consult when confronted with an octogenarian whose marital partner has just died after 50 years of intimate companionship. Similar challenges are faced by counselors who differ markedly from their clients in ethnicity and general life experience.

The elderly person's own perspective has been less well represented in the otherwise useful literature on suicide and other self-destructive behaviors. Why does this imbalance exist? I think it is because several salient characteristics of the high-risk elderly person are also characteristics that reduce the likelihood of open and substantive communication:

1. Living alone, for example, obviously reduces the opportunities to express and explain suicidal intent to a caring person.
2. Residing in a low-income, transient urban area tends to make a person socially invisible (Baum, Deckel, & Gatchel, 1982): There may be few contacts with people who are in a position to recognize suicidal intent and take some constructive action.
3. The depressive state frequently associated with suicidality often has the effect of reducing communication—and of actually driving other people away. Few seek out the company of elderly people who express such negative affects as bitterness or apathy.
4. The fact that most suicides in old age are committed by men suggests that reluctance to seek help may be strongest among those elders who are at greatest risk. It has been shown (Stroebe, Stroebe, & Dommitner, 1988; Stroebe & Stroebe, 1989–1990) that, among bereaved elders, men are less likely to accept opportunities to discuss their situation and generally enter into fewer interpersonal relationships. Furthermore, the men appear to suffer even more than the women, although this suffering is less likely to be recognized by others. It is probable that a similar gender difference would also emerge if a parallel study could be conducted on suicidality. And, of course, there might also be a more direct link between unrelieved suffering during bereavement and suicide among elderly men.

Moreover, our awareness of the elderly suicidal person's own perspective has been dimmed by a lack of wholehearted effort on the part of caregivers and researchers. Society's response to the emotional and behavioral problems of its elderly citizens has been undercut by inadequate financing, lack of training and manpower, and poor coordination among service systems (Hinrichsen, 1990). These are all palpable manifestations of the low priority that our society has so often given to elderly people, as well as to the persistent reluctance of professionals to face challenges related to loss and death (Kastenbaum, 1964).

It might be useful, then, to offer separate overviews of death and suicide in old age from the observer's and the experiencer's perspective. This will be followed by a few suggestions regarding the integration of both perspectives.

The Observer's Perspective

Numbering Our Days

Statistics have a strong influence on the observer's perspective. The basic data themselves are well known and do not require extensive treatment here. However, some of their implications deserve immediate attention.

Fact: Morbidity and mortality increase with advancing adult age. For example: cardiovascular disease in white men rises from a mortality rate of 3.9 in youth (ages 15 to 24), to 265.8 at midlife (45 to 54), and to 5,407 in old age (75 and older). The rate of cancer mortality among black females increases from 5.1 in youth, to 211.8 at midlife, and to 859.8 in old age (Gee, 1989a). The overall mortality rate (Table 1) in the United States leaves no doubt that death rides on the shoulders of age (Gee, 1989b).

Implications: The external observer is justified in associating advancing age with morbidity and death. Indeed, it would be difficult to avoid this

TABLE 1.   All-Cause Mortality Rate by
Age Group, 1985

Age group	Female	Male
Youth	0.5	1.4
Midlife	3.9	6.9
Old age	52.0	85.4
Very old age (85+)	140.1	170.8

association. However, one must still decide what to make of the age/death linkage, a question that will grow in complexity as additional facts are introduced.

Fact: Men are at greater risk for death across the life span. This trend has already been illustrated. It begins with infancy and continues through to the most advanced age levels. Furthermore, mortality reduction has been greater for women in all industrialized nations throughout the twentieth century.

Implication: The high suicide rate among elderly males (highest of all age/gender combinations) should be interpreted within the framework of all-cause mortality. Taken by itself, suicidal behavior does occur with relatively greater frequency among old males as compared with everybody else. But considered as just one cause of mortality among many, suicide follows the general contours we have already seen: higher death rates with age and among males.

Fact: Suicide is a less dominating cause of death among old people. The three leading causes of death in youth are outcomes of human error or malice: accident, homicide, and suicide. By contrast, elderly adults are vulnerable to many diseases and degenerative conditions. The suicide rate among old-age white males is less than 1 per cent of the death rate for cardiovascular disease. Even though the all-ages suicide rate is highest for old-age white males, this constitutes a relatively small fraction of the all-cause mortality, because elderly people face so many other life-threatening conditions.

Implication: It may be wiser to consider suicide within the context of total risk to life among older people. Most young people will continue to grow older, but all aged people will die, even if there is never another act of suicide. In contemplating suicide, the young, the middle aged, and the old person might well be influenced by their differential perceptions of probable life expectancy. A young athlete leaps to death because she cannot bear the thought of going on "forever" with the shame and frustration of having finished second in a race. An old man restricted to bed-and-chair existence growls that "This is some life, isn't it!" Suicide would be a ridiculous option, though, because "Any day now, I'll wake up and find myself dead, so what's the point?"

The "gerontosuicidologist," therefore, must be a "deathologist" as well. Suicide can be quite a different option for the healthy youth who might otherwise live another 80 years and the ailing octogenarian whose days on earth would be numbered even without a self-destructive intervention.

Facts: (a) There are more elderly people alive today (both in actual numbers and proportion of population) than ever before, but (b) continued survival traps the individual within a continuously dwindling subpop-

ulation. These facts are both related and disjunctive. The first refers to the "greying" of America and other industrialized societies. Our interpretation of death, suicide, and aging is conditioned by the age distribution within the general population. Being relatively few, old people tended to be valued more highly in preliterate societies. Being numerous, in industrialized societies, old people tend to be seen as competing for resources.

The second point brings to mind the sociological contention that people become at greater risk for suicide when they belong to subpopulations that are diminishing in size (Maris, 1981). Age has not usually been considered within this context, but it does seem to qualify: Just growing older guarantees that one will have fewer peers and implies that one may also lose the benefits associated with reference group interactions. The longer we survive, the more marginal we become as part of a cohort that is continuously decimated by age-associated mortality. Only one of every two white males born 75 years ago remains alive: This circumstance doubles the effective suicide rate when the original cohort is used as the reference group (Kastenbaum, in press-a). With every passing year, the survivor becomes more and more marginal from the standpoints of peer reference, support, and communication. Whether or not this decreasing cohort factor actually does influence suicide rate is a question that should be resolved by further research.

Implications: Society in general will become increasingly aware of the age–death–suicide linkage, because elderly people are becoming a more substantial proportion of the population. But society (including social and health care professionals) may not sufficiently recognize the mixed picture of (a) the hardy, survivorship qualities of old people, and (b) the isolating effect of relentless loss of peers. Elderly people are old because they have survived, and they have survived, in part, because of biological and psychosocial characteristics that contribute to effective coping. Despite the relatively high suicide rate in old age, the obvious fact that these people have survived into old age suggests that their viability and allegiance to life should not be underestimated.

How Policy Makers Construct Age, Death, and Suicide

Some of the most influential of all external perspectives are those held by our society's policy makers, the people who determine the allocation of resources, access, and opportunity. Their implicit constructions of age, death, and suicide are highly consequential: For example, will aged men and women find it increasingly easy or more difficult to obtain hearing aids, utilize public transportation, and maintain a telephone in their homes? For elderly people trying to manage on a fixed and limited income, there can be substantial consequences associated with an unfavorable pattern of resource allocation. These consequences occur at both the pragmatic and the perceptual/symbolic levels.

Pragmatic. A widow or widower, living alone, cannot afford the type of hearing aid that would prove effective. Communicational and interactive opportunities are also restricted by a lack of convenient and affordable transportation—and now the individual must even consider the possibility of giving up telephone service in order to stay within budget. This set of restrictions would probably be only part of a larger pattern. The overall effect would be detrimental to morale, contributing to social isolation and depression which, in turn, tends to impair nutritional intake and general preservation of health status.

Perceptual/Symbolic. The same person develops the impression that society does not care much whether he or she thrives or suffers, lives or dies. The response may take the form of an increase in anger and paranoid tendencies or an intensification of self-doubt and blame. Either way, the elderly person is likely to interpret a pattern of unavailable resources and opportunities as a negative message from society.

Combining both levels of response, the affected elderly people are likely to engage in fewer social interactions, become increasingly isolated, and be at greater risk for a variety of health problems. For every person who commits suicide, a much larger number will have lapsed into a dysphoric and unproductive mode of life or will have experienced excessive stress in attempting to struggle against their predicament. To put it another way, how policy makers construe the role of old people in society and society's obligations to the aged tends to create a milieu that either supports or undermines the individual's viability.

For a closer look at the policy maker's construction of old age, death, and suicide, let us consider one of the most influential of recent books in this area. In *Setting Limits* (1987), Daniel Callahan addressed the difficult problem of "medical goals in an aging society." Most subsequent discussions have traced their roots to Callahan's analysis and recommendations. Callahan has opened a valuable dialogue and offered a number of observations that deserve serious consideration. Having said that, I must add that I am appalled by both his logic and his conclusions.

Callahan proceeds on the assumption that a modern (or, if you prefer, postmodern) society does not have the resources to provide all the health care that might be desired by all its citizens. Elderly people deserve a share, but it must be closely monitored and controlled, otherwise this growing subpopulation will drain funds that should be used for other purposes. Callahan's intention is to provide an ethical framework for a workable medical resource allocation program.

Callahan's views on suicide and euthanasia (1987) are presented within the framework of his revised conception of the human life course. Three basic principles are offered (italics in the original):

1. After a person has lived out a natural life span, medical care should no longer be oriented to resisting death.
2. Provision of medical care for those who have lived out a natural life span will be limited to the relief of suffering.
3. The existence of medical technologies capable of extending the lives of the elderly who have lived out a natural life span creates no presumption whatever that the technologies must be used for that purpose (pp. 171–173)

These principles are united by the concept of "a natural life span (NLS)." Death is said to be acceptable when we have completed our NLS. Callahan supports this idea by asserting that all cultures have developed models in which death loses its negative meaning and destructive power when it occurs at the end of a life that has been lived "properly and fully." Therefore, it follows that society is justified in withholding "death-resistant" interventions from people who have completed their full and proper lives. One can imagine computer banks automatically disenfranchising large numbers of men and women every day as they reach the established age limit—no doubt on a birthday.

Callahan realizes that suicide and euthanasia or assisted suicide might arise as popular options, should his plan win acceptance. If society decides not to keep people alive beyond some agreed-upon age, then some physically impaired people, confronting this bleak nonfuture, could decide to give death a hand. But, according to Callahan, they mustn't! Suicide, assisted suicide, euthanasia—any form of voluntary self-cessation—would be wrong. Why? Because to sanction self-cessation would be to establish "a special benefit for the aged." There is no reason to allow this favor to old people, since we do not approve of younger people killing themselves when life becomes difficult. Furthermore, death would become so attractive that a great many of the "young old" would also rush to do themselves in.

To find this view persuasive, one needs to accept "natural" as a clear, objective, universal, and value-free concept. I have found just the opposite: that "natural" has been one of the loosest and most abused of concepts, made to serve many divergent causes—a weasel word among weasel words. One would also have to accept chronological age as an acceptable marker for determining rights, privileges, and opportunities. This type of thinking has been roundly condemned by the community of gerontological scholars and practitioners who frequently comment on the lack of predictive value that is associated with chronological age (e.g., Hayslip & Panek, 1989). Even the Federal government, after years of foot dragging, has removed the mandatory retirement requirement for college professors and a number of other workers (a measure that is scheduled to become operative in 1994). As research findings along a broad front continue to subordinate chronological age to more substantive variables (e.g., personality, coping style, social support group, health genetic factors), what Callahan offers is a wildly regressive proposition.

Furthermore, there is a serious blurring of perspectives in the contention that this approach is justified because all (?) cultures hold that death loses its negative meaning when it comes at the end of a full and proper life. The error comes in substituting a self-protective societal reflex for knowledge of the individual's own thoughts, feelings, and wishes. The passing of old people often has a tranquillizing effect on society at large because it suggests that Death is playing the game by the rules we would like to see respected: Take the old and leave us and our young alone (Kastenbaum, in press-b). However, as we will see below, there is a great diversity among old people themselves as they balance between life and death. One could enforce the proposed rules only by avoiding the eyes and voices of aged peole who still have strong and vital attachments to life.

Finally, in Callahan's scenario, a catch-22 situation would be imposed. People who had completed their "natural life span" would be expected to accept death as proper—yet they would not have the right to take the smallest voluntary step toward cessation. Waiting to die would be the normative role for the very old person, and the ideal role player would be passive and silent or, to put it more bluntly, impersonating a corpse.

Perhaps the most striking feature of this proposal is simply the fact that it was offered by an eminent ethicist and greeted warmly by many policy makers. A plethora of assumptions are made about what would be beneficial to aged people and what life-and-death choices they should have made for them. Absent is any interest in discovering and reflecting upon the older person's own views in all their richness and diversity.

The Experiencer's Perspective

Enough has been learned about the older person's attitudes toward dying, death, and suicide to caution against rigid and sweeping generalizations. People bring a variety of distinctive life experiences with them into old age. Moreover, they function in a variety of ongoing situations. "This is the best time of our lives!" is what we hear—and

believe—from some hard-working and responsible couples who now
finally have the opportunity to pursue their own interests in a sunny
clime. By contrast, the nearly immobile nursing home resident responds
with averted eyes and flattened voice to a visitor: "You want to talk
to me? Nobody talks to me. I'm nobody. I don't even talk to myself any
more." Although it would be easier for the suicidologist to proceed on
the assumption that all elderly people have one characteristic orientation
toward life and death, this would be an unjustified indulgence.

How Elderly People Face Death

When given the opportunity to express themselves by words and
action, elderly people reveal a diversity of attitudes toward death and
dying. There are a few themes and characteristics that appear with
some frequency, but one learns to attend carefully to the individual's
perspective rather than make stereotypical assumptions.

A pioneering study by J. M. A. Munnichs (1966) in the Netherlands
revealed much that would be found later in the United States (e.g.,
Weisman & Kastenbaum, 1970) and Australia (Kellehear, 1990; Kellehear & Lewin, 1988–1989). Munnichs' interviews with 100 men and
women over the age of 70 revealed diversity first and foremost. A
distinctive configuration of thoughts, feelings, and attitudes could be
developed for each respondent. Fear did not dominate. Relatively few
people were apprehensive about dying, and fewer still were obsessed
by the idea of death and finitude. A fairly large group (30%) "were
incapable of attaching any significance to the end, preferring to evade
or ignore the issue" (Munnichs, 1966, p. 124). As an overall trend, most
of the elders had worked out some kind of accepting orientation toward
death, while a significant minority adeptly practiced one form of evasion
or another.

Munnichs further observed that the most common attitude was one
of familiarity. Death was no longer a threatening stranger or a mysterious
external force. Instead, it might almost be said that death had become
a piece of mental furniture that was just going to remain there, whether
one cared much for it or not. People who had developed this attitude
were able to form a new equilibrium, situating themselves a little
further away from both life and death (if I read Munnich's data and
interpretations correctly). In other words, many older people had, indeed,
become "philosophical" about death.

Weisman and Kastenbaum (1970) used the psychological autopsy
approach to reconstruct the lives and deaths of hospitalized geriatric
patients in the United States. Despite the methodological and national

differences, they also found that anxiety was not the predominant response to the prospect of dying and death. Two psychological patterns were almost equally prevalent. About half the 120 patients had engaged in a gradual withdrawal and "closing down operations" as death approached—but nearly as many had continued to pursue their customary daily activities within days or hours of their demise. One woman was quite explicit about it: "Death wants me—he'll have to find me at Bingo!" The abundance of information provided by the psychological autopsy approach revealed that many elderly patients had taken practical or symbolic actions in anticipation of their deaths, for example, giving away their favorite pipe and tobacco to a buddy or embroidering one's name on a pair of underpants ("So my drawers will have a happy afterlife, the next gal will know whose drawers are warming her bottom"; this from a 93-year-old who was convinced that she herself would have no afterlife and who did, in fact, die the day after completing the embroidering project). Again, as with the Munnich study, one was continually impressed by the diversity of individual attitudes toward death, even though a few general patterns also emerged. (Kubler-Ross, 1969, "stages of dying" definitely did not emerge; the ego integration hypothesis of Erikson, 1959, and the life review theory of Butler, 1964, were, rather, consistent with the pattern of findings.)

Two recent studies from Australia have also extended, as well as confirmed, previous investigations. Most of the 100 dying people studied by Kellehear and Lewin (1988–1989) found some way to take leave of their family and friends. For example, one elderly woman made a large number of miniature dolls that she gave to people on their last visit. Some preferred to do their leave-taking fairly early, while they still felt in command of themselves, but others preferred to exchange last words and sentiments as close as possible to the very end.

In this predominately late-middled-aged and elderly sample, age did not seem to be as important as personality style, social support system, and factors directly associated with the terminal illness. The desire and the opportunity to affirm personal relationships through a leave-taking process may have helped to control anxiety and reduce impulses toward ending one's life through suicide, assisted suicide, or euthanasia. As with the geriatric patients, these men and women also engaged in a number of instrumental activities in anticipation of death (e.g., seeing to their wills and bequests).

In a later report from the same sample, Kellehear (1990) found that most of the terminally ill people engaged in some form of personal preparation for death, for example, talking about funeral arrangements, making special arrangements for funds, etc. There seemed to be an implicit conception of the "good death" that emphasized looking after the needs of the survivors in a practical manner. Religious concerns were subordinated to material preparations, especially in the preterminal phase. Although religious interest became more prominent as people moved closer to death, the predominant concern remained with making practical arrangements and doing what they could to make things easier for their survivors.

None of the studies mentioned above found suicidality to be a dominant theme, although the participants were elderly men and women and, in many, cases, already experiencing their terminal illness. Perhaps the most promising avenue for exploring the relatively low orientation toward self-destruction would be to follow up on phenomena noted in all of the studies. Many of the endangered people came up with their own compensatory strategies. There may have been periods of anxiety, confusion, and depression as they first absorbed the impact of disability, loss, and foreshortened futurity. After doubting and suffering, many adjusted effectively to their changed and changing situation.

My colleagues and I had an exceptionally good opportunity to observe this adjustment process while providing clinical services and conducting research in a geriatric hospital. Anger, despair, and suicidality were more characteristic of this population than of the independently living elders studied by Munnichs, Kellehear, and some others. Much of this negative affect, however, arose from painful conditions of life rather than the prospect of death. Although there were multiple sources of distress and multiple types of response, the confrontation–adjustment process can be illustrated by Angela H. Just past her 79th birthday, Mrs. H. was admitted to the geriatric facility at the request of her children and the family physician. She raged, wept, and turned her face to the wall (literally). Mrs. H. refused to eat and resisted the sympathetic approaches of hospital personnel. Gradually it became clear that she had two primary sources of concern: (a) sense of abandonment by her family—a perceived loss of love and lack of gratitude, and (b) overwhelming alarm at seeing herself among so many other old and infirm people. "Just let me die. That's all I want," was one of the few statements she would offer.

Yet, Mrs. H. survived and even thrived. Within about 6 weeks she had emerged from her social withdrawal and discarded the wish to die. What had taken place? One of our more thorough multidisciplinary team efforts resulted in (a) eliminating a painful infection, thereby making it easier for her both to sleep and to move about, and (b) encouraging family visits (despite Mrs. H.'s initial unreceptivity), including the first great-grandchild and a favorite cat. But it was Mrs. H. herself who turned the corner from depression to renewed engagement with life. Recognizing the improvement in her physical condition, she (grudgingly) took more interest in the hospital environment. There she discovered that there were a number of lively people about, including a gentleman toward whom she once had an unrequited romantic attachment. Without relinguishing the right to complain about hospital food and other disagreeable facets of life, Mrs. H. became the center of her own little social circle and enjoyed more companionship than had come her way in a long time.

Many other elderly people also passed through the ordeal of displacement from home and admission to a geriatric facility, and eventually found their own way to continue a meaningful life. I have thought of Mrs. H. in particular because one afternoon I happened to be sitting with her group at their favorite table in The Captain's Chair (our tavernesque drinking-and-complaining place). They were buzzing about the news that a retired public official had just committed suicide because of poor health. Mrs. H. remained silent for a few minutes and then pronounced her verdict: "The only thing he ever did was to make bad things worse. He was stupid young and stupid old!" She then reached for her second jelly doughnut.

Toward an Informed and Empathetic Perspective

What would be the ideal perspective on death and suicide in old age? We might disagree considerably on the details, but it is likely that we agree that the views of the elderly person should themselves be well represented and enhanced by the insights that can be contributed from an informed observer. And—to put it the other way around—what we would hope to avoid is the rigid application of stereotyped assumptions.

Here are a few of the possible components for an informed and empathetic perspective:

1. The fact that elderly men and women often can accept the inevitability of death with a sense of composure does not mean that they have had enough of life. Rosa Lee, an uneducated woman dying of cancer, speaks for many others when she tells a doctoral student: "There's gonna be death. So long as you don't be born you won't have to die. But the minute you're born, you can die just anytime . . . And it don't worry me to know what I have, and to know what I'm gonna die of" (Zinker, 1966, p. 159). What Rosa Lee does worry about are the stressful and restrictive conditions of her life. Given a little relief and a little comfort, she would prefer to keep going.

2. Advanced age, infirmity, and the prospect of death do not necessarily lead to a high lethality or suicidality orientation. If there are ways to improve the situation, if there are alternatives, many people will find

them. The perceptive and empathic observer will help endangered people to discover and employ alternative strategies. Often this assistance will take the form of avoiding counterproductive interventions, that is, heavy sedation that destroys judgment and initiative while confirming fears of loss of efficacy. Ida C., for example, was an 85-year-old, stroke-disabled widow who had to give up a beautiful home to enter a care facility many miles away from her children. Yet when asked, "Do you think you might be better off dead?" she replied with astonishment. "The very idea. What, be buried in the ground. I have time for that" (Richman, 1991, p. 165). Ida C.'s outspoken humor would have not been available to her had she become a casualty of overmedication.

3. As death is not invariably the most demoralizing enemy for the elderly person, so suicide is not invariably the most demoralizing form of death. Philosopher G. C. Prado (1990) offers a thoughtful analysis of "surcease suicide," while, from the clinical perspective, I have encountered numerous examples of self-cessation that embodied many characteristics that are often associated with the "good death" (Kastenbaum, 1976). This does not mean that suicide in old age is to be encouraged and preventive efforts abandoned. But it does suggest that we understand and respect the frame of reference that makes suicide seem a relatively attractive option to a person who has survived many a previous crisis.

4. As a society, there is no time better than the present for examining our own mixed feelings toward and messages to elderly men and women. I am especially concerned about public policy approaches (such as "setting the limits") that place a veneer of rational cost–benefit verbiage over a devaluation of the aged and a fear of contact with those whose mortality can no longer be denied.

These are but a few starting points for a project that has a long, long way to go: recognizing and coming to terms with the old man or woman inside each of us.

References

Baum, A., Deckel, A. W., & Gatchel, R. J. (1982). Environmental stress and health: Is there a relationship? In G. S. Sanders & J. Suls (Eds.), *Social psychology of health and illness* (pp. 279–306). Hillsdale, NJ: Erlbaum.

Butler, R. N. (1964). The life review: An interpretation of reminiscence in the aged. In R. Kastenbaum (Ed.), *New thoughts on old age* (pp. 265–280). New York: Springer.

Callahan, D. (1987). *Setting limits.* New York: Simon and Schuster.

Erikson, E. H. (1959). Identity and the life cycle. *Psychological Issues, 1,* 18–164.

Gee, E. (1989a). Causes of death. In R. Kastenbaum & B. K. Kastenbaum (eds.), *Encyclopedia of death* (pp. 38–41). Phoenix: Oryx Press.

Gee, E. (1989b). Mortality rate. In R. Kastenbaum & B. K. Kastenbaum (Eds.), *Encyclopedia of death* (pp. 183–185). Phoenix: Oryx Press.

Hayslip, B., & Panek, P. E. (1989). *Adult development and aging.* New York: Harper & Row.

Hinrichsen, G. (1990). *Mental health problems and older adults.* Santa Barbara, CA: ABC-CLIO.

Kastenbaum, R. (1964). The reluctant therapist. In R. Kastenbaum (Ed.), *New thoughts on old age* (pp. 139–145). New York: Springer.

Kastenbaum, R. (1976). Suicide as the preferred way of death. In E. S. Shneidman (Ed.), *Suicidology: Contemporary developments* (pp. 425–441). New York: Grune & Stratton.

Kastenbaum, R. (1991, April 17). *Suicide and the elderly: Some unanswered questions.* Presented at the American Association of Suicidology, Boston.

Kastenbaum, R. (in press-a). Suicide among elderly Americans: A sociocultural perspective. In H. Radebold & R. Schmitz-Scherzer (Eds.), *Suicide in old age.* Darmstaat, West Germany: Steinkopf.

Kastenbaum, R. (in press-b). *The psychology of death.* New York: Springer.

Kellehear, A. (1990). *Dying of cancer.* London: Harwood.

Kellehear, A., & Lewin, T. (1988–1989). Farewells by the dying: A sociological study. *Omega, Journal of Death and Dying, 19,* 275–293.

Kubler-Ross, E. (1969). On death and dying. New York: Prentice-Hall.

Maris, R. W. (1981). *Pathways to suicide.* Baltimore: Johns Hopkins University Press.

Munnichs, J. A. A. (1966). Old age and finitude. New York: S. Karger.

Prado, C. G. (1990). *The last choice: Preemptive suicide in advanced age.* New York: Greenwood Press.

Richman, J. (1991). Suicide and the elderly. In A. A. Leenaars (Ed.), *Life span perspectives of suicide* (pp. 153–170). New York and London: Plenum Press.

Stroebe, W., Stroebe, M. S., & Domittner, G. (1988). Individual and situational differences in recovery from bereavement: A risk group identified. *Journal of Social Issues, 44,* 143–158.

Stroebe, M. S., & Stroebe, W. (1989–1990). Who participates in bereavement research? A review and empirical study. *Omega, Journal of Death and Dying, 20,* 1–30.

Weisman, A. D., & Kastenbaum, R. (1970). *The psychological autopsy: A study of the terminal phase of life.* New York: Behavioral Publications.

Zinker, J. C. (1966). *Rosa Lee.* Painesville, OH: Lake Erie College Press.

2

Epidemiology of Suicide in the Elderly

John L. McIntosh, PhD
Indiana University at South Bend

ABSTRACT: Suicide rates in the United States and most other countries are higher among the elderly than among the population as a whole. Typically, rates peak in older adulthood. Epidemiological data for the current levels and trends in suicide among the elderly are presented with a focus on United States figures. Age, sex, race, marital status, and methods of suicide as factors in suicide among the old are detailed, followed by a discussion of past trends and future predictions of changes in elderly suicide rates. In addition to fatal suicidal behaviors, the data and literatures on parasuicide and survivors of elderly suicide are briefly noted.

The fastest growing population has for some time been older adults. This trend is expected to continue and even accelerate in the future as the "baby boomers" reach old age and birth-rate trends and medical technological advances allow larger proportions of the population to reach late life. An increase in the size of elderly populations is observed and is expected in North America and in much of the world. With the growth of elderly individuals in the population, the need to determine present and possible future aspects of self-destruction in this group becomes increasingly important.

Epidemiological and demographic considerations of suicidal behavior attempt to determine the levels of suicidal behavior among a population or subpopulation, characteristics of those who are at high and low risk for suicidal actions, as well as the changing nature of self-destructive behavior. The emphasis here will be to elucidate the levels, trends, and characteristics with respect to suicide among the older adult population. An accurate portrayal of elderly suicide, however, can only be

Address correspondence to John L. McIntosh, PhD, Department of Psychology, Indiana University at South Bend, P.O. Box 7111, South Bend, IN 46634; (219) 237–4343.

obtained by placing suicide among our elders in the context of suicidal behavior in the population as a whole and other subgroupings. With these issues in mind, the high risk of older adults for suicide will be presented. In the presentation of data herein, the "elderly" or "older adult" population will be defined as those 65 yeas of age and above. This definition implies no absolute delineation at the age of 65, and in fact, arguments for when an individual is considered "elderly" may vary widely (e.g., 50 and above, 60 and above, etc.). The age of 65 is utilized to allow historical comparability of data, particularly in the context of the Social Security legislation in the 1930s that indirectly established this chronological age as a "definition" of elderly.

As with other age groups, self-destructive behavior in older adults is displayed in direct and overt fashion by such behaviors as death by suicide as well as by attempted suicide (also known as parasuicide). Additionally, older adults exhibit covert and less direct forms of suicidal behavior (also called indirect self-destructive behavior or subintentioned death; see Farberow, 1980; Shneidman, 1973), e.g., failure to follow medical regimens and self-starvation. An additional aspect is the group of survivors who remain alive following the death of a loved one by suicide. Vital statistics are maintained only for death by suicide, and these will be the primary focus of this presentation. Research findings with respect to attempted suicide will be reviewed, and a preliminary consideration of the epidemiology of survivors of elderly suicide will also be advanced. Indirect forms of self-destruction have not been widely studied, although it has been suggested that, among older adults, their number almost certainly exceeds that of direct suicidal behavior (Kastenbaum & Mishara, 1971; for a review, see McIntosh & Hubbard, 1988).

Completed Suicide/Official Statistics on Suicide: United States

Mortality statistics are collected, compiled, published, and available from governmental agencies (in the United States, this agency is the National Center for Health Statistics, Mortality Branch). Although official suicide statistics have been criticized with respect to bias and underreporting (Douglas, 1967, Ch. 23; Lester, 1972, Ch. 12), the evidence is not undisputed (Sainsbury & Jenkins, 1982). Although such official figures are undoubtedly not a totally accurate representation of the numbers that occur, they may be viewed as the most conservative estimates (Allen, 1984), and it should be pointed out that they are the only systematically available data. The mortality statistics presented below will focus on the United States. However, the risk of suicide among the elderly relative to other population groups within a particular culture is more similar than dissimilar with respect to other cultures, despite tremendous variability between cultures with respect to overall suicide rates (Ruzicka, 1976; Shulman, 1978).

In another vein, the use of official statistics, which are nearly always in the form of grouped or aggregated data, has the limitation of representing groups but not necessarily the individuals therein. That is, although official statistics may indicate which aggregate groupings display high risk of suicide, they may lead us to inaccurately assign high (or low) risk to individual cases (this issue has been referred to as the "ecological fallacy"). Clinical experience and skills must be utilized in individual assessment of suicide risk. Although demographic data may provide some gross indications of risk, they should not be utilized as a replacement for clinical judgment on an individual level. Therefore, although, as will be noted below, females in older adulthood are at much lower overall risk of suicide than elderly males as a group, not only do women commit suicide in late life, but the risk of suicide may be great for a particular elderly female.

Current Levels

At the present time in the United States, there are approximately 30,000 deaths annually officially recorded as suicide. Among these suicides, more than 6000 are by older adults. In 1988, the most recent year for which final official data are available, there were 30,407 U.S. suicides, and 6,363 were committed by Americans aged 65 and above. In other words, there was a suicide, on the average, every 17.3 minutes in the United States in 1988, with an elderly American dying by suicide every 83 minutes. Alternatively, of the 83 suicides per day, 17 were aged 65 and above (National Center for Health Statistics [NCHS], 1990; some 1988 data reported here were obtained directly from NCHS prior to their eventual publication in the 1988 volume of *Vital Statistics of the United States*).

It is often stated in literature on the elderly that suicides are over-represented among older adults. That is, the "old" comprised 12.4% of the U.S. population in 1988 (United States Bureau of the Census, 1990) but they accounted for 20.9% of the suicides. By way of comparison, the young (15 to 24 years of age) represented 15.2% of the population and 16.2% of the suicides (4,929 in 1988), a nearly equal representation. The largest *number* of suicides actually occur among the adult population aged 25 to 44 or 25 to 64. However, either of these two age groupings comprise a large segment of the U.S. population as well. For 1988, the group aged 25 to 44 acounted for 32.1% of the population and 39.2% of the suicides (for 25 to 64, the figures were 50.8% and 62.0%, respectively).

A more revealing and accurate way to understand suicide risk is to calculate *rates* of suicide rather than considering the raw number of suicides by age or any other group. A suicide rate is determined by dividing the number of suicides in a population or subpopulation by the number of individuals in that same population or subpopulation and multiplying by a constant number. The constant most often employed is 100,000, such that the rate of suicide indicates the risk of suicide per each 100,000 unit of population. Therefore, the rate allows a measure of risk that takes into account the number of individuals who contribute to the number of suicides. This makes the rates directly comparable across subpopulations, while numbers may not be comparable (the misleading nature of numbers compared to rates can be seen clearly, e.g., in the case of marital status, as noted below).

The rate of suicide in the United States as a whole was 12.4 per 100,000 population in 1988, compared to 21.0 per 100,000 elderly Americans (the rate for the young, 15 to 24 years of age, was 13.2). Older adults, therefore, are at a risk of suicide that exceeds the rates for the nation (and the young) by more than 50%. As can be seen in Figure 1, the rate for older adults has always exceeded the national rates by at least this margin and, in fact, by much more in earlier decades.

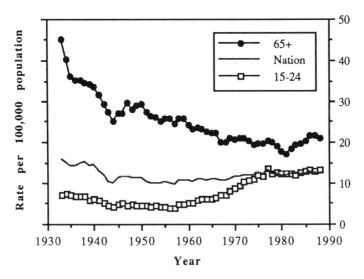

Figure 1.   Elderly Suicide in the United States, 1933–1988

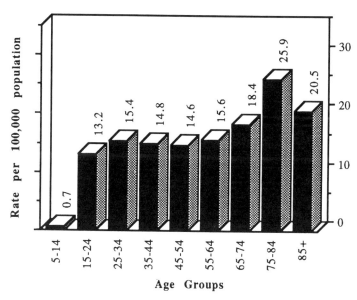

Figure 2.   Suicide Rates by Age: United States, 1988

Suicide rates by age reveal a pattern that may best be described as increasing with age (although a flatter pattern may be seen for the young adult periods prior to a higher peak in older adulthood), such that the highest rates are observed after the age of 65. Indeed, Figure 2 shows that the rate of suicide is higher for each elderly age group than for any of the age groupings below 65.

A closer look at Figure 2 reveals that suicide rates are highest among the old-old (those 75 years of age and above) and slightly lower among the young-old (those aged 65 to 74 years). It should be noted, however, that the rates among even the young-old exceed all other younger-aged groups. Gerontologists have also made recent differentiations among the old-old, with the extremely old being further delineated (Rosenwaike, 1985). For the nation as a whole, these oldest of the older adult population (85 years of age and above in these data) represent high risk for suicide, although this risk is slightly lower than for the 75 to 84 age group and remains higher than any other age grouping, including the young-old, 65 to 74 (the comparison of 75 to 84 to 85 and older is greatly influenced by sex differences, see below). Higher rates among the old-old are particularly important for future aspects of elderly suicide, because this is the fastest growing subpopulation of older adults.

The age pattern of Figure 2 masks the more accurate risk of groups that combine to produce the total population figures. Notable and most consistent among these demographic factors are sex, race, marital status, and methods of suicide. As for suicide in general, the single demographic variable with the greatest predictive power is sex. As can be seen in Figure 3, males and females display differential levels of suicide risk throughout the lifespan, and the characterization of the pattern by age is also distinct for each sex. Male suicide rates exceed those for females at all ages. Male rates of suicide increase with age and reach their highest levels in the oldest age grouping, whereas female rates increase with age (but always at noticeably lower levels than for males), peak in middle adulthood (the 40s to 50s, most often 45 to 54), and decline slightly with advancing age. Because male rates continue to rise throughout older adulthood while female rates decrease, the differential in rates continues to rise throughout older adulthood while female rates decrease, the differential in rates for the sexes is greatest during old age (and least different in middle age, where female rates peak). The 1988 rate for males 65 and above was 41.9, compared to 6.6 for elderly females (this compares to 20.1 and 5.0 in males and females of the population as a whole, respectively). Therefore, although the number of females exceeds the number of males in the population of older adults, the rates of suicide (and the numbers as well in this case, 5,170 suicides by males and 1,193 by females 65 and above in 1988) are markedly higher among elderly males.

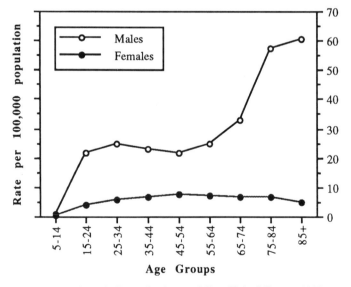

Figure 3. Suicide Rates by Age and Sex: United States, 1988

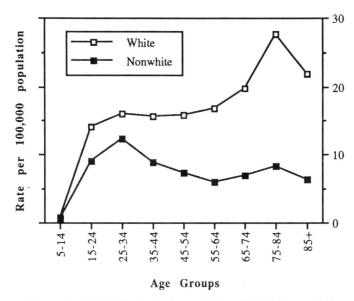

Figure 4.   Suicide Rates by Age and Race: United States, 1988

Racial differences in older adulthood, like differences by sex, tend to be at their greatest in older adulthood. Rates for the white population increase with age, peaking in older adulthood as noted above for the nation as a whole (see Figure 4). Nonwhite suicide rates, on the other hand, peak in young adulthood (generally by the age of 35) and decline to low levels in older adulthood. White suicide rates in older adulthood for 1988 were 22.4, while those for nonwhites were 8.3 (compared to 13.4 and 6.8 for each group in the nation as a whole, respectively).

Combining race with sex shows that males of both races are at higher risk than females of either race, although whites exhibit higher suicide rates than their same-sex counterparts among nonwhites in each case. White males above age 65 have the highest rates of suicide (45.0 in 1988), followed by nonwhite males (13.9), white females (6.9), and finally nonwhite females (4.4). While these rate differentials are similar to those in the nation as a whole for each race-sex group (21.7, 11.4, 5.5, 2.6, respectively), the differences are highest in old age.

Although whites display higher rates than for nonwhites as a whole, there are distinct ethnic differences among and between the groups that comprise the nonwhite as a whole category (McIntosh & Santos, 1981). Population data to calculate rates for ethnic minorities are only consistently available for census years. McIntosh (1985, 1986) compiled data from official sources by age for the 3-year period 1979 to 1981 for each racial/ethnic minority for which national data were available. Tremendous variability was observed in overall rates, even among those groups that could be characterized similarly with respect to suicide rates by age. Overall, with all ages combined, highest rates were noted for Native Americans (13.6), followed, in decreasing order, by whites (12.9), Japanese-Americans (9.1), Chinese-Americans (8.3), Blacks (5.7), and Filipino-Americans (3.6). Among these groups, suicide rates peaked in young adulthood among both Native Americans and blacks and declined to low rates among older adults. Similar to the nation as a whole and whites, peaks in suicide among the elderly were observed for Chinese-, Japanese-, and Filipino-Americans. The suicide rates for those aged 65 and older were 28.7 for Chinese-Americans, 19.2 for whites, 18.3 for Japanese-Americans, and 9.3, 6.2, and 3.6 for Filipino-Americans, blacks, and Native Americans, respectively. In a study of ten states for which suicide data for Hispanics were available, McIntosh (1987b) found rates that were generally similar to those for blacks when all ages were combined and lower than for Whites as a whole (most Hispanics are white and would be included in the white aggregate data with Anglos). Also similar to blacks, Hispanic suicide rates peaked in young adulthood and were low in old age (rate of 10.4 for 1979 to 1981 among those Hispanics aged 65 and above; overall rate of 7.5). Therefore, although suicide data often combine all nonwhites and other minorities into a single category, the great heterogeneity within that grouping should be recognized.

Another demographic variable that has shown a reliable pattern is the marital status of the deceased. Although the number of suicides is much greater among the married in the population as a whole as well as in older adulthood, most of both population groups are married. Therefore, when the rates of suicide are calculated, the married display the lowest risk among the marital status categories. The divorced and widowed exhibit the highest rates of suicide, with the single (never married) population generally falling between the married and marital disruption groups. The greater risk of suicide in the elderly is nonetheless quite apparent when comparing older adulthood to the nation as a whole (except among the widowed). As can be seen in Table 1 for 1988, the rate of suicide in each marital category except the widowed is higher for the corresponding older adult group than for the nation (calculated for the population 15 and above; population figures employed in the calculation of rates are from United States Bureau of the Census, 1989), and the rate differential is particularly marked for males.

Finally, the methods employed to commit suicide also exhibit age-related patterns. Although firearms have been used in the most deaths by suicide for nearly all groups in the United States (McIntosh &

TABLE 1. United States Suicide Rates by Marital Status and Sex: Elderly[a] and National Rates[b], 1988

Marital Status	Both Sexes Combined		Males		Females	
	Nation	Elderly	Nation	Elderly	Nation	Elderly
Total[c]	16.0	22.3	26.4	43.7	6.4	7.1
Married	11.5	20.6	18.7	32.1	4.5	5.3
Single (never married)	18.2	25.5	28.2	54.7	6.2	7.4
Widowed	21.8	21.4	84.7	87.2	9.0	8.1
Divorced	36.6	46.5	66.2	101.7	15.7	12.8

Population source: U.S. Bureau of the Census (1989)

[a] "Elderly" refers to age 65 years and above.

[b] Note: Because the population data differ for this table and the other figures in the text (U.S. Bureau of the Census, 1990), rates for elderly will differ in the two locations. Similarly, the utilization of different population estimates as well as defining "total" as age 15 and above will produce differing rates for national data as well. Other than comparisons among these tabled data, figures in the text are most comparable to traditionally available official data. Rates for all tables and in text are per 100,000 population.

[c] "Total" refers to age 15 and above.

Santos, 1982; tremendous cultural differences exist in this regard, e.g., see McIntosh, in press-a), the proportion of suicides attributable to firearms is greater among the elderly than for any other age group (McIntosh & Santos, 1985–86). For instance, in the United States population as a whole in 1988, firearm use was top-ranked and represented 59.8% of all suicides (18,169 of 30,407 suicides), compared to 67.0% of the elderly suicides in the same year (4,264 of 6,363). Hanging, another highly lethal method, ranks second for the elderly and for the nation (11.9% compared to 14.4%, respectively). Gas and solid or liquid poisons represented the largest proportions of the remaining suicides after firearms and hanging, with the old utilizing both methods less frequently than observed in the nation as a whole.

When considering suicide methods, however, differences by sex are large (McIntosh & Santos, 1981, 1985–86). For females in the population as a whole, firearms have become the most often utilized method (39.7%), exceeding the historical preference for solid or liquid poisons (27.0%). Although this reversal of traditional patterns among elderly females was not observed by McIntosh and Santos (1985–86) for data through 1978, by 1988 the same pattern for females in the nation as a whole is noted (24.2% by solid/liquid poisons compared to 31.9% by firearms). For males, firearms are overwhelmingly highest at all ages, and the proportions for elderly males exceed those for all other age groups (proportions for elderly males by firearms were 75.1%, compared to 65.0% for males of all ages combined). It should be noted that, although both males and females in older adulthood utilized firearms most often, the use of solid and liquid poisons was markedly higher among females compared to males (24.2% vs. 3.1%).

A distillation of the above data would produce a picture of modal or highest risk for suicide in the elderly (keeping in mind the issues of the ecological fallacy noted above). This individual would be an old-old, white male who is divorced or widowed and uses a firearm to kill himself. Although this does not represent the only older adult at high risk for suicide, by demographic variables alone, these factors are associated with high likelihood of death by suicide.

Trends

Past and Recent Trends. Returning for a moment to Figure 1, it can be clearly seen that, in the long term, rates of suicide among the old have declined dramatically. In fact, the decreasing tendency in suicide among the elderly has been of longer duration (beginning in the 1930s) than the more recent increases observed among the young (beginning in the 1950s), and the decrease of more than 50% in that time period is as dramatic as the over 200% increase for young people. From the extremely high rates among older adults during the economically depressed 1930s (rates of approximately 35–40 per 100,000 population), the rates have declined to around 20 for the 1980s (compared to rates of approximately 4 to 13 per 100,000 for young people in the 1950s and the late 1970s–80s, respectively; national rates have remained between 10 and 13 since 1941 after being between 14 and 15 per 100,000 during the 1930s).

Although the best characterization of long-term trends in elderly suicide rates is one of decline, short-term trends are upward. Following 1981, the year in which the lowest recorded rate for older adults (17.1) since the United States government began keeping mortality records in 1900 was observed, suicide rates for those 65 and above increased every year through 1987 and decreased minimally for 1988 (by comparison, during the period following 1977 and through 1988 the rates for those aged 15 to 24 years has remained stable or somewhat lower). During this 7-year time period from 1981 to 1988, the rate of elderly suicide increased more than 25% (while the number of elderly suicides increased by more than 40%). The implications of these short-term trends for future levels of elderly suicide are unclear (see below), but in recent years older adults have become slightly more likely to commit suicide and a several-decade downward trend has been apparently reversed or at least halted or slowed.

As demonstrated in Figure 1, the decline of suicide rates in the elderly is of long standing, yet minimal attention has been given to explanations or even recognition of its occurrence. McIntosh (1984) showed that the declines in rates were almost exclusively produced by decreased risk among elderly males, with elderly females showing stable to slight declines over time. It was also revealed that lower rates were the result largely of trends for elderly whites, as nonwhite elderly rates changed little. Similarly, McIntosh further found that rate declines were greater for the young-old than for the old-old.

Explanations for the long-term declines in elderly suicide have led to speculations with respect to the possibly positive influence of access to hospitals associated with Medicare, elderly political and social activism (e.g., the Gray Panthers and AARP), improved elderly social services (Ford, Rushforth, Rushforth, Hirsch, & Adelson, 1979), use of antidepressants (Busse, 1974), changing attitudes toward retirement (Kruijt, 1977), and particularly increased economic security. The latter has been implicated in at least two correlational studies of elderly white males (Marshall, 1978; McCall, 1991). Holinger and Offer (1982) found no relationship between the increasing number of elderly adults and the suicide rate of older adults, although McIntosh, Hubbard, and Santos (1980) observed a significant correlation between the sex ratio and suicide rates for the old. That is, the increased numbers of older adults was not simply related to the decrease in rates; but the increasing number of women relative to men in older adulthood was. No studies of the recent increases in rates have been made, but McIntosh (in press-b) has speculated that decreases in feelings of economic security among older adults might be a factor.

Future Trends. As considered elsewhere (McIntosh, in press-b), there have been predictions that elderly suicide in the future will be extremely high, based on the large number of members in the "baby boomer" cohort and the higher rates of suicide exhibited by this cohort compared to earlier cohorts at the same ages (Manton, Blazer, & Woodbury, 1987; Pollinger-Haas & Hendin, 1983). The sole issue considered in these predictions has been the size of the cohort and the resultant effects on their social and psychological well-being. On the other hand, McIntosh (in press-b) has argued that the size of the baby boomer cohort across their adult lives may actually work to their benefit and potentially result in more attention and resources dedicated to the needs of older adults. This would logically produce lower rather than higher rates of suicide. Additionally, the higher rates of suicide by baby boomers at younger ages may reduce the number remaining alive in this cohort who are prone or susceptible to suicide when they reach older adulthood, which would also lower suicide rates. It is contended that the future among older adults is not certain, and it is more likely that events and measures taking place during the next several decades will have the potential to significantly increase or decrease the risk of suicide among the elderly of the next century.

Completed Suicide/Official Statistics on Suicide: International Data

Outside of the United States, many other cultures compile and make available mortality statistics. The World Health Organization (WHO) collects these figures from contributing nations and publishes them in regular reports. The most recent figures (WHO, 1991) are generally for the years 1988 or 1989 (although earlier years are all available in some cases). Before proceeding to a brief consideration of these figures and the extent of elderly suicide in countries other than the United States (for more detailed reviews of suicide in various cultures see Diekstra, 1990; Farberow, 1975; Kruijt, 1977; Tousignant & Mishara, 1981), a few comments should be made regarding cross-cultural statistical comparisons and comparability. The issues of bias and underreporting mentioned above are appropriate here, as well, with additional problems such as different systems of death certification procedures and political and cultural factors that might affect death certification among the various nations represented. Therefore, some caution should be exercised in strict and direct comparison of rates from culture to culture. The statements that follow are based on the available international data.

Current Levels

As can be seen in Table 2 and Figure 5, suicide rates vary widely worldwide. The United States is among countries with a national suicide rate in the moderate range. As was noted above for the United States, elderly rates of suicide are with only one exception (Scotland) higher than for the nation as a whole, among the nations for which data are available. While patterns of rates of suicide by age have long been observed to be somewhat variable across countries (e.g., Ruzicka, 1976), just as for the United States, suicide rates most often display a peak in late adulthood among the countries who report figures to the WHO (1991). Also similar to information presented above, males rates of suicide in old age (defined once again here as age 65 and above) are virtually without exception markedly higher than those observed among elderly females (in both China and Japan, rates are high for both sexes and, although male rates exceed those for females, the differences are much less than generally seen for other cultures; see Table 2).

Trends

Full information about trends would require annual data for the elderly of each of the nations represented. Such a presentation is beyond the scope of the present effort, although a crude indication of trends may be obtained by comparing the currently available levels of suicide among elderly males and females with an earlier compilation by Ruzicka (1976). In that article, Ruzicka (p. 410) presents a table of rates for males and females aged 65 to 74 years around the year 1970. If the nations reporting figures in the WHO (1991) report around the year 1988 are similarly categorized as one measure of changes in rates over time, a consideration of the current and Ruzicka's categorized rates (by increments of 10 per 100,000 population for male rates (i.e., 0–9.9, 10.0–19.9, . . . 70.0 and over; and 5 per 100,000 for female rates, that is, 0–4, 5.0–9.9, . . . 30.0 and over) shows that many countries displayed

TABLE 2. International Suicide Data: National and Elderly Rates (per 100,000 population)

Country	All Ages Combined (National Data)			Older Adults (65+ Years of Age)			Year
	Total	Males	Females	Total	Males	Females	
Hungary	41.6	61.4	23.1	83.8	127.2	56.8	1989
East Germany	25.8	36.1	16.3	70.6	119.7	47.6	1989
Sri Lanka	35.8	48.8	22.3	57.6	92.6	18.5	1985
China	17.1	14.7	19.6	57.1	63.2	52.0	1989
Bulgaria	16.2	23.5	9.2	50.0	76.8	29.0	1989
Austria	24.9	36.1	14.7	48.5	82.2	30.6	1989
Yugoslavia	16.2	22.4	10.2	47.2	74.9	28.6	1988
Denmark	26.0	33.3	19.0	43.8	55.8	34.5	1988
France	20.8	30.2	11.7	43.8	74.2	24.2	1988
Japan	17.3	21.5	13.1	43.1	49.7	38.7	1989
Czechoslovakia	17.7	27.1	8.8	39.5	67.8	21.9	1989
Switzerland	22.8	32.8	13.2	38.9	64.9	21.7	1989
U.S.S.R.	19.5	30.9	9.4	36.6	64.5	25.7	1988
West Germany	16.5	23.5	10.0	32.2	55.0	20.5	1989
Finland	28.3	46.2	11.6	32.1	62.4	15.8	1988
Uruguay	8.5	12.9	4.2	25.5	45.4	10.6	1987
Argentina	7.5	10.8	4.2	24.0	43.9	9.0	1986

Country							Year
Israel	6.2	8.9	3.6	23.4	33.3	14.8	1987
United States	12.4	20.1	5.0	21.0	41.9	6.6	1988
Italy	7.6	11.1	4.4	20.5	35.7	10.4	1988
Puerto Rico	7.7	13.5	2.1	20.3	39.4	3.8	1987
Portugal	7.2	11.0	3.7	20.1	35.7	9.3	1989
New Zealand	14.0	22.2	6.0	18.9	34.2	7.8	1987
Netherlands	10.3	13.2	7.5	18.6	28.6	12.0	1988
Spain	7.1	10.7	3.7	18.6	30.8	10.2	1986
Australia	13.3	21.0	5.6	18.4	31.8	8.5	1988
Norway	16.8	24.5	9.3	18.1	28.5	10.6	1988
Canada	13.5	21.4	5.9	15.2	27.7	6.2	1988
Poland	11.3	19.3	3.7	14.3	27.2	6.5	1989
Venezuela	4.1	6.6	1.5	11.3	22.2	2.1	1987
England & Wales	7.4	11.2	3.7	10.2	16.0	6.3	1989
Scotland	10.4	15.4	5.6	9.7	15.4	6.2	1989
Ireland	7.5	11.0	4.0	9.4	16.4	4.1	1988
Greece	4.0	5.9	2.3	8.8	11.7	6.5	1988
Ecuador	4.6	6.3	2.8	8.2	14.9	2.5	1988
Colombia	3.8	6.0	1.6	5.7	11.9	0.7	1984

Source: WHO (1991); rates for 65 years of age and above as well as both sexes combined ("Total") were calculated from figures included in tabled material in WHO (1991). The countries included here are all those for which at least 20 suicides total occurred among those aged 65 years of age and above.

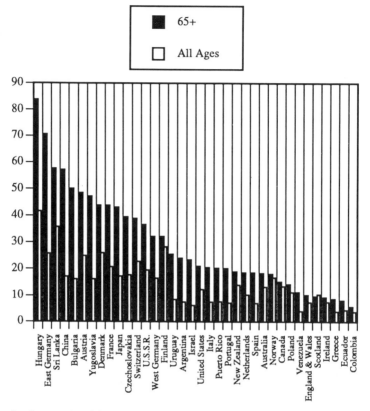

Figure 5. International Suicide Data: National and Elderly (65+ Years of Age) Suicide Rates

no categorical change in rates for either elderly males or females aged 65 to 74 years (e.g., Scotland, Canada, Italy, Poland, Netherlands, USA, Hungary), while several countries each experienced declines for both sexes (e.g., England and Wales, Portugal, Australia, New Zealand, West Germany, Japan, Czechoslovakia) or increases for both sexes (e.g., Ireland, Norway, Bulgaria, Yugoslavia, Sri Lanka). The other countries of this report displayed either some mixed rate changes (one sex increased, the other decreased; e.g., Greece, France) or a combination of change for one sex of older adults but no change for the other (e.g., Northern Ireland, Israel, Switzerland, Denmark, Finland, Austria). The net conclusion of this comparison is that little great change in the overall levels of elderly suicide occurred in the countries available and that no single trend in elderly suicide has occurred in all or most nations of the world in the last two decades. However, it must be concluded that, the elderly are at high risk for suicide in all the cultures compared to their national levels.

Attempted Suicide/Parasuicide

While official national figures are available for deaths by suicide, no such data are maintained on a national level for nonfatal suicidal actions. These intentional actions, that are similar to suicide completions but do not result in death, are referred to most often as attempted suicides, although the term parasuicide is becoming increasingly utilized (Kreitman, 1977). The lack of consistently maintained figures forces reliance on epidemiological studies conducted by researchers in specific locations (i.e., cities, hospitals, etc.). Although there is not the variety of information for various demographic variables and trends noted above, the research has produced relatively consistent results for age and sex differences.

Attempted suicide is often expressed as a ratio of attempted to completed suicides. In this manner, Shneidman (1969) and others (Wolff, 1970) have suggested what seem to be conservative estimates for the population as a whole of somewhere between 8 and 20 attempts for each completed suicide. Figures based on research findings for young people have resulted in ratios of 200:1 (McIntire & Angle, 1981) to as high as 300:1 (Curran, 1987). Among the elderly, on the other hand, the ratio is more often estimated at 4:1 (Stenback, 1980). These extreme differences in ratios suggest that relatively speaking, when an older adult attempts suicide, the likelihood of the action ending fatally are high (when compared to the young in particular). Similar conclusions result from the literature that calculate rates of attempted suicide by age. These studies (for reviews, see Kreitman, 1977; Weissman, 1974; Wexler, Weissman, & Kasl, 1978) find that attempted suicide rates, unlike completed suicide rates, peak in the young and decline to much lower levels with increasing age, such that older adults have the lowest rates of attempted suicide across the life span.

Once again, sex differences are so dramatic that the most revealing picture emerges when this variable is examined for attempted suicide. Both in the population as a whole and in all age groups (including older adulthood), attempted suicide is most prevalent among females. Contrary to completed suicide rates, attempted suicide rates are markedly higher among women of all ages, although the differences between males and females tend to be greatest among the young and lessen among the elderly (but remaining nonetheless higher for women). The findings of an old study demonstrate the differences noted here. Schmid

and Van Arsdol (1955) calculated the proportion of those who completed
suicide from among those who attempted for cases in Seattle from 1948
to 1952. They observed that, for the full sample, 30.7% of those who
attempted suicide actually died, with female proportions much lower
than among males (15.1% vs. 46.5%). For young people aged 20 to 29,
the proportion was only 14.7% overall, while female and male figures
were 7.5% and 26.4%, respectively. By contrast, the proportion among
older adults (aged 60 and above) was 62.9% for both sexes combined,
and 38.2% of the elderly females compared to 67.8% of the elderly
males who died when they attempted suicide. Therefore, the number
and rates of suicide attempts are much higher among the young and
much lower among the old of both sexes. However, the probability that
an attempt will end fatally increases with age. One interesting implication of these data, because there are many more attempts than completions, is that females actually exhibit a greater number of total
suicidal behaviors (nonfatal attempts combined with completions) than
do males at all ages.

Survivors of Elderly Suicide

A final, usually omitted aspect of the demography of elderly suicide
concerns the individuals who remain alive to grieve the loss through
suicide of an elderly loved one. Until recently, little attention has
focused on this aspect of suicide, and the few investigations of elderly
survivors of suicide have focused almost exclusively on widows (Farberow,
Gallagher, Gilewski, & Thompson, 1987; see also McIntosh, 1987a; for
an overview of the literature on survivors, see Dunne, McIntosh, &
Dunne-Maxim, 1987). No systematic epidemiological or demographic
study has been conducted to determine the number of survivors of
suicide generally or among any particular age group. One estimate of
the number of survivors for each suicide was advanced by Shneidman
(1972) in the foreword to Albert Cain's landmark book *Survivors of
Suicide*. Shneidman suggested that there were six survivors for each
suicide and, in the absence of a better estimate, this figure will be
utilized here. If Shneidman is correct, the approximately 6,000 official
suicides each year among older adults produce an annual figure of
36,000 survivors. Over time, the cumulative number of individuals
who must grieve and mourn the suicide death of a loved one becomes
sizable. This population of individuals is faced with possibly altered
grieving and mourning practices and experiences that accompany this
mode of death. Both the number of such potentially at-risk individuals
and their grieving experiences remain to be accurately determined,

but they represent an additional toll that accompanies any consideration of the extent to which suicidal behavior is an important issue among any particular group.

In summary, older adults are the highest risk group for death by suicide. The demographic subgroups at the greatest risk among American elderly are males, the widowed or divorced, the old-old, and whites. Although rates of attempted suicide are lower than at younger ages, the risk to life that an attempted suicide represents to an older adult makes attention to actual or threats of suicidal actions crucial. Suicide is an important mental health problem among older adults at present, and efforts to alleviate factors associated with suicidal behaviors need to be addressed to prevent potentially increased levels of suicide among the large numbers of older adults of the future.

References

Allen, N. (1984). Suicide statistics. In C. L. Hatton & S. M. Valente (Eds.), *Suicide: Assessment and intervention* (2nd ed., pp. 17–31). Norwalk, CT: Appleton-Century-Crofts.

Busse, E. W. (1974). Geropsychiatry: Social dimensions. In G. J. Maletta (Ed.), *Survey report on the aging nervous system* (DHEW Publication No. [NIH] 74-296, pp. 195–225). Washington, D.C.: United States Government Printing Office.

Curran, D. K. (1987). *Adolescent suicidal behavior*. New York: Hemisphere.

Diekstra, R. F. W. (1990). An international perspective on the epidemiology and prevention of suicide. In S. J. Blumenthal & D. J. Kupfer (Eds.), *Suicide over the life cycle: Risk factors, assessment, and treatment of suicidal patients* (pp. 533–569). Washington, D.C.: American Psychiatric Press.

Douglas, J. D. (1967). *The social meanings of suicide*. Princeton: Princeton University Press.

Dunne, E. J., McIntosh, J. L., & Dunne-Maxim, K. (Eds.). (1987). *Suicide and its aftermath: Understanding and counseling the survivors*. New York: Norton.

Farberow, N. L. (Ed.). (1975). *Suicide in different cultures*. Baltimore, MD: University Park Press.

Farberow, N. L. (Ed.). (1980). *The many faces of suicide: Indirect self-destructive behavior*. New York: McGraw-Hill.

Farberow, N. L., Gallagher, D. E., Gilewski, M. J., & Thompson, L. W. (1987). An examination of the early impact of bereavement on psychological distress in survivors of suicide. *Gerontologist, 27*, 592–598.

Ford, A. B., Rushforth, N. B., Rushforth, N., Hirsch, C. S., & Adelson, L. (1979). Violent death in a metropolitan county: II. Changing patterns in suicides (1959–1974). *American Journal of Public Health, 69*, 459–464.

Holinger, P. C., & Offer, D. (1982). Prediction of adolescent suicide: A population model. *American Journal of Psychiatry, 139*, 302–307.

Kastenbaum, R., & Mishara, B. L. (1971, July). Premature death and self-injurious behavior in old age. *Geriatrics, 26*, 71–81.

Kreitman, N. (1977). *Parasuicide*. New York: Wiley.

Kruijt, C. S. (1977). The suicide rate in the Western world since World War II. *Netherlands Journal of Sociology, 13*, 54–64.

Lester, D. (1972). *Why people kill themselves: A summary of research findings on suicidal behavior*. Springfield, IL: Thomas.

Manton, K. G., Blazer, D. G., & Woodbury, M. A. (1987). Suicide in middle age and later life: Sex and race specific life table and cohort analyses. *Journal of Gerontology, 42,* 219–227.

Marshall, J. R. (1978). Changes in aged White male suicide: 1948–1972. *Journal of Gerontology, 33,* 763–768.

McCall, P. L. (1991). Adolescent and elderly White male suicide trends: Evidence of changing well-being? *Journal of Gerontology: Social Sciences, 46,* S43–S51.

McIntire, M. S., & Angle, C. R. (1981). The taxonomy of suicide and self-poisoning—A pediatric perspective. In C. F. Wells & I. R. Stuart (Eds.), *Self-destructive behavior in children and adolescents* (pp. 224–249). New York: Van Nostrand Reinhold.

McIntosh, J. L. (1984). Components of the decline in elderly suicide: Suicide among the young-old and old-old by race and sex. *Death Education, 8*(Suppl.), 113–124.

McIntosh, J. L. (1985, November). *Suicide among minority elderly.* Paper presented at annual meeting of the Gerontological Society of America, New Orleans, LA.

McIntosh, J. L. (1986, April). *Cross-ethnic suicide: U.S. trends and levels1.* Paper presented at the annual meeting of the American Association of Suicidology, Atlanta, GA.

McIntosh, J. L. (1987a). Survivor family relationships: Literature review. In E. J. Dunne, J. L. McIntosh, & K. Dunne-Maxim (Eds.), *Suicide and its aftermath: Understanding and counseling the survivors* (pp. 73–84). New York: Norton.

McIntosh, J. L. (1987b, May). *Hispanic suicide in ten U.S. states.* Paper presented at the joint meeting of the American Association of Suicidology and the International Association for Suicide Prevention, San Francisco, CA.

McIntosh, J. L. (in press-a). The methods of suicide. In R. W. Maris, A. L. Berman, J. Maltsberger, & R. Yufit (Eds.), *Assessment and prediction of suicide.* New York: Guilford.

McIntosh, J. L. (in press-b). Older adults: The next suicide epidemic? *Suicide and Life-Threatening Behavior.*

McIntosh, J. L., & Hubbard, R. W. (1988). Indirect self-destructive behavior among the elderly: A review with case examples. *Journal of Gerontological Social Work, 13,* 37–48.

McIntosh, J. L., Hubbard, R. W., & Santos, J. F. (1980, November). *Suicide among nonwhite elderly: 1960–1977.* Paper presented at the meeting of the Gerontological Society of America, San Diego, CA.

McIntosh, J. L., & Santos, J. F. (1981). Suicide among minority elderly: A preliminary investigation. *Suicide and Life-Threatening Behavior, 11,* 151–166.

McIntosh, J. L., & Santos, J. F. (1982). Changing patterns in methods of suicide by race and sex. *Suicide and Life-Threatening Behavior, 12,* 221–233.

McIntosh, J. L., & Santos, J. F. (1985–86). Methods of suicide by age: Sex and race differences among the young and old. *International Journal of Aging and Human Development, 22,* 123–139.

National Center for Health Statistics. (1990). Advance report of final mortality statistics, 1988. *NCHS Monthly Vital Statistics Report, 39*(7, Suppl.).

Rosenwaike, I. (1985). *The extreme aged in America: A portrait of an expanding population.* Westport, CT: Greenwood.

Pollinger-Haas, A., & Hendin, H. (1983). Suicide among older people: Projections for the future. *Suicide and Life-Threatening Behavior, 13,* 147–154.

Ruzicka, L. T. (1976). Special subject: Suicide, 1950 to 1971. *World Health Statistics Report, 29*(7), 396–413.

Sainsbury, P., & Jenkins, J. S. (1982). The accuracy of officially reported suicide statistics for purposes of epidemiological research. *Journal of Epidemiology and Community Health, 36,* 43–48.

Schmid, C. F., & Van Arsdol, M. D., Jr. (1955). Completed and attempted suicides: A comparative analysis. *American Sociological Review, 20,* 273–283.

Shneidman, E. S. (1969). Prologue: Fifty-eight years. In E. S. Shneidman (Ed.), *On the nature of suicide* (pp. 1–30). San Francisco: Jossey-Bass.

Shneidman, E. S. (1972). Foreword. In A. C. Cain (Ed.), *Survivors of suicide* (pp. ix–xi). Springfield, IL: Thomas.

Shneidman, E. S. (1973). *Deaths of man.* New York: Quadrangle.

Shulman, K. (1978). Suicide and parasuicide in old age: A review. *Age and Ageing, 7,* 201–209.

Stenback, A. (1980). Depression and suicidal behavior in old age. In J. E. Birren & R. B. Sloane (Eds.), *Handbook of mental health and aging* (pp. 616–652). Englewood Cliffs, NJ: Prentice-Hall.

Tousignant, M., & Mishara, B. L. (1981). Suicide and culture: A review of the literature (1969–1980). *Transcultural Psychiatric Research Review, 18,* 5–32.

United States Bureau of the Census. (1989). Marital status and living arrangements: March 1988. *Current Population Reports,* Series P-20, No. 433.

United States Bureau of the Census. (1990). United States population estimates, by age, sex, race, and Hispanic origin: 1980 to 1988. *Current Population Reports,* Series P-25, No. 1045.

Weissman, M. M. (1974). The epidemiology of suicide attempts, 1960 to 1971. *Archives of General Psychiatry, 30,* 737–746.

Wexler, L., Weissman, M. M., & Kasl, S. V. (1978). Suicide attempts 1970–1975: Updating a United States study and comparisons with international trends. *British Journal of Psychiatry, 132,* 180–185.

Wolff, K. (1970). Observations on depression and suicide in the geriatric patient. In K. Wolff (Ed.), *Patterns of self-destruction: Depression and suicide* (pp. 33–42). Springfield, IL: Thomas.

World Health Organization. (1991). *World health statistics annual 1990.* Geneva: Author.

3

Social and Economic Correlates of the Elderly Suicide Rate

David Lester
Center for the Study of Suicide
Bijou Yang
Drexel University

ABSTRACT: A review of research found that the suicide rates of the elderly show similar regional social correlates as the suicide rates of younger groups and that these rates can be explained using similar sociological theories. Time-series studies in the USA indicate that the impact of economic prosperity on the suicide rate of the elderly is beneficial, whereas the impact on the suicide rate of younger adults is detrimental. The issues raised by this research are discussed.

Although the statistical rarity of suicide makes individual acts of suicide difficult to predict; social suicide rates are very stable. For example, Lester (1987) found that the suicide rates of a sample of European nations in 1875 were quite similar to their suicide rates one hundred years later, though there were, of course, exceptions. On the other hand, suicide rates vary considerably between different demographic groups within a society. For example, the suicide rate of those aged 15 to 24 in the USA in 1960 was only 5.2 per 100,000 per year, while the suicide rate of those aged 65 or older was 24.3. By 1987, the suicide rate of those aged 15 to 24 was 12.9, while the suicide rate for those aged 65 to 74 was 19.4; for those aged 75 to 84, 25.8; and for those aged 85 or more, 22.1. (For more detailed epidemiological trends, see McIntosh, this issue.)

Despite the stability of social suicide rates, there are also gradual changes in the suicide rates over time of the whole society and of the

For correspondence, contact David Lester, RR41, 5 Stonegate Court, Blackwood, NJ 08012.

different demographic groups. In recent years, the United States has witnessed an increase in the suicide rate of youths, for example, from 5.2 in 1960 to 12.9 in 1987. Interestingly, these trends are not found in all nations. During the 1970s for example, several nations—such as Japan and Sweden—experienced a decrease in youth suicide rates, while others—such as Australia and Norway—experienced an increase (Lester, 1988a).

The stability of the social suicide rates provides an intriguing focus for the social scientist, therefore. Is it possible to identify correlates of the social suicide rate and, in particular for the present paper, for the suicide rate of the elderly?

This question may be answered in several ways. First, the focus can be on regional variations in the suicide rate of the elderly, such as variations over U.S. states and over nations, or on time-series variation, such as the variation of the elderly suicide rate during the last 50 years in the United States. Second, we may distinguish between different types of correlates, such as demographic correlates (for example, the proportion of the elderly in the population), social correlates (for example, the divorce rate of the society), and particular subsets of the social correlates that are of special interest to the society (e.g., the state of the economy).

Regional Studies

Nations

Stack (1981) explored the social correlates of sucide rates in 37 nations of the world in 1970. In a multiple regression analysis, he found that the suicide rates of elderly men and women were positively related to the divorce rate and negatively to the square of the divorce rate. The suicide rates of the elderly were not related to the percentage of Roman Catholics in the population. This result was observed for those aged 55 to 64 as well as those aged 65 to 74. This pattern of results was similar to that for the total suicide rate of the nations. The relationship between divorce rates and the suicide rates implies that the relationship is a polynomial one. When divorce is more common in a society, the suicide rate is higher, but each unit change in the divorce rate brings about a smaller change in the suicide rate until, at high levels of divorce, the slope of the curve is negative. Stack saw his results as confirming Durkheim's theory (1897) that social integration (in this instance marital integration) is related to the suicide rate for the societal suicide rate in general and for the elderly suicide rate in particular.

American States

Durkheim's (1897) classic theory of suicide in societies was based on two dimensions. Suicide was hypothesized to be common in societies in which the degree of social integration (that is, the strength of the individual's social network) was very low (egoistic suicide) or very high (altruistic suicide). Similarly, suicide was hypothesized to be very common where the degree of social regulation (that is, the degree to which the individual's attitudes and desires are regulated by the society) was very low (anomic suicide) or very high (fatalistic suicide).

Lester (1988b) sought to test Durkheim's theory using the American states in 1980 by subjecting a large number of socioeconomic variables to a factor analysis in order to identify the variables having strong intercorrelations with one another. He identified seven factors (*clusters* of variables), one of which appeared to tap social integration, since it had high loadings from such individual variables as the divorce rate, interstate migration, church attendance, and alcohol consumption.

Lester (1991) then examined the correlations between the scores of each state on these seven factors and the suicide rates of the different age groups in the USA. The results are shown in Table 1. It can be seen that the suicide rates of almost all of the age groups were associated with the social disintegration factor (Factor II). Where social disintegration was higher, the suicide rates of most of the age groups were also higher. In addition, many of the suicide rates were associated with the age factor (Factor III). The younger the population in a state, the higher the suicide rate for many of the age groups—both young and old, it should be noted. Furthermore, both the suicide rates of those aged 15 to 24 and those aged 75 to 84 were associated with the southern factor (Factor IV). The suicide rates of youths and of the elderly were lower in Southern states. Thus, Lester concluded that the social correlates of elderly suicide rates in the United States were similar to those of adult and youth suicide rates.

Similarities in the correlates of the suicide rates of both young and old were observed in a study of the effects of state handgun control laws on suicide rates in 1970. Lester (1983, 1984) found that states with stricter handgun control laws had lower rates of suicide, and this result held true for the suicide rates of each age group, both young and old.

TABLE 1. Correlations of Factor Scores with Suicide and Homicide Rates

Age				Factor			
	I	II	III	IV	V	VI	VII
Males							
15–24	-0.05	0.57[a]	-0.28[a]	-0.32[a]	-0.01	-0.11	0.12
25–34	0.16	0.58[a]	-0.34[a]	-0.05	-0.27[a]	0.09	0.11
35–44	-0.10	0.64[a]	-0.19	0.01	-0.09	0.14	-0.04
45–54	-0.25[a]	0.52[a]	-0.27[a]	0.04	0.06	-0.04	-0.09
55–64	-0.21	0.38[a]	-0.28[a]	0.03	-0.02	-0.17	-0.21
65–74	-0.22	0.50[a]	-0.48[a]	0.01	0.03	-0.02	-0.32[a]
75–84	-0.15	0.53[a]	-0.38[a]	-0.24[a]	0.10	-0.04	-0.12
85+	-0.14	0.26[a]	0.13	0.01	0.09	0.20	-0.01
Females							
15–24	0.01	-0.05	-0.04	-0.17	0.16	-0.10	-0.11
25–34	0.09	0.73[a]	-0.01	0.16	0.14	-0.06	-0.01
35–44	0.08	0.63[a]	-0.09	-0.13	0.17	-0.02	0.19
45–54	0.12	0.49[a]	-0.40[a]	-0.10	-0.08	-0.14	-0.11
55–64	0.01	0.31[a]	-0.21	-0.13	-0.12	-0.11	0.11
65–74	0.21	0.52[a]	-0.24[a]	0.07	-0.07	0.14	-0.02
75–84	0.37[a]	-0.05	-0.07	0.06	-0.33[a]	0.01	0.14

From Lester, 1991. Factor labels: Factor I urban/wealth; Factor II social disintegration; Factor III age; Factor IV Southernness; Factor V labor force participation; Factor VI unemployment; Factor VII Roman Catholicism

[a] significant at the 5% level or better

American Counties

Pescolsolido and Wright (1990) examined the effects of divorce on the suicide rates by age at the county level in the United States, looking at both age-specific divorce rates and the overall divorce rates of the counties. For men, they found that the age-specific divorce rate has a beneficial effect on the suicide rate of young men (aged 18 to 24), an aggravating effect for middle-aged men (aged 45 to 64), and a negligible effect for men aged 25 to 44 and elderly men (aged 65 and older). For women, the effect of divorce on suicide was negligible except for elderly women, for whom the effect was beneficial. In contrast, the overall level of divorce in the counties generally had a detrimental effect on the suicide rates of both sexes at most ages. The age-specific presence of children had a protective effect for both young women (18 to 24 years old) and elderly women (65 years and older) and a deterimental effect for middle-aged women, particularly for those 45 to 64.

This study shows the usefulness of looking at age-specific social indicators as well as overall measures of the social indicators. The two types of measures gave very different results in Pescosolido and Wright's study.

Time-Series Studies

Yang (1990) analyzed the impact of socioeconomic variables on different age groups from 1940 to 1984 in the United States. She examined the impact of the gross national product per capita, the unemployment rate, the participation of women in the labor force, the divorce rate, and the percentage of the population that is Roman Catholic on the suicide rates of various demographic groups.

Yang entered both the current value of the gross national product per capita and the value in the previous year into the multiple regression. The total impact of the gross national product per capita on the suicide rate, therefore, would be the sum of these two components. If the sum of these two terms is negative, economic prosperity has a beneficial effect on the suicide rate. If the sum of the two terms is positive, then economic prosperity has a detrimental impact on the suicide rate.

Her results are summarized in Table 2. She identified two features in the association between the economic environment and suicide rates in different age groups: (1) economic prosperity seemed to have a detrimental impact on the suicide rate of younger adults (those aged 15 to 44) and a beneficial impact on the suicide rates of older adults (those

TABLE 2. Results of Multiple Regressions for Suicide Rates of Different Age Groups in ihe United States, 1940–1984 (regression coefficients)

Age	GNP/cap	Lagged GNP/cap	Unemployment rate	Female labor force participation	Divorce rate	Roman Catholicism
15–24	1.66[a]	−1.36[a]	0.04[a]	−0.02[a]	1.04[a]	0.07[a]
25–34	1.71[a]	−0.92[a]	0.04[a]	−0.03[a]	0.59[a]	0.04[a]
35–44	0.84[a]	−0.71[a]	0.01[a]	−0.03[a]	0.51[a]	0.05[a]
45–54	0.25[a]	−0.26[a]	0.01[a]	−0.03[a]	0.21[a]	0.04[a]
55–64	0.06	−0.37[a]	0.00	−0.02[a]	0.14[a]	0.02[a]
65+	−0.27[a]	−0.34[a]	0.01	−0.00	0.03	−0.01[a]

[a] Regression coefficient statistically significant at the 5% level or better.
From Yang, 1990.

aged 45 and older), and (2) the unemployment rate had an impact on suicide rate only for those aged 54 or younger.

One striking feature of the results that differentiates the older adults is that the social variables seemed to have less of an impact on their suicide rates than did the economic variables. The only variable with a significant role in the multiple regression for the elderly suicide rate was membership in the Roman Catholic Church. The higher this membership, the lower the suicide rate of the elderly.

Greater economic prosperity usually implies a better social infrastructure, which includes the basic services and facilities needed for the growth and functioning of a community. This should improve the quality of life for the elderly in a variety of ways, but the specific mechanisms of how economic prosperity leads to this require further study.

When the suicide rates of the elderly were examined separately for men and women, Yang observed that the suicide rate of elderly women was more responsive than the suicide rate of elderly men to social variables such as female labor force participation and the divorce rate. However, for the suicide rates of both elderly men and women, Roman Catholic Church membership did not play a significant role.

Yang also broke down the elderly suicide rate by race and observed that (1) the suicide rate of the nonwhite elderly was associated with female labor force participation while the suicide rate of the white elderly was not, and (2) the association between Roman Catholic Church membership and the suicide rate was significant for both groups but with opposite impacts. The impact was beneficial for the white elderly suicide rate but detrimental for the nonwhite elderly suicide rate.

The general conclusions appear to be that the effects of economic variables on suicide rate may be stronger in younger adults than in older adults past retirement age, and that these effects are negative for the young and positive for the elderly. Times of economic prosperity are associated with higher suicide rates in younger adults and lower suicide rates in elderly adults. It is important to note that the results of time series regression analyses often vary with the period chosen. Thus, it will of interest to extend these analyses to the late 1980s and early 1990s as data for these years become available, especially since the late 1980s were supposedly times of economic prosperity and the early 1990s times of economic hardship.

Demographic Shifts

Holinger (1987) looked at the United States from 1933 to 1982 and found that, as the proportion of youths (aged 15 to 24) in the population increased, the suicide and homicide rates for this group also increased. For older Americans, a negative correlation was observed, that is, as the proportion of older Americans increased in the population, their suicide and homicide rates decreased. Holinger and Lester (1991) have largely replicated these time-series results in a regional study of the United States.

Holinger explained these results using Easterlin's (1980) proposal that a large cohort may lead to increased competition for relatively fewer resources, especially among youths in the society. Thus, these youths will experience higher rates of unemployment, fewer educational opportunities, and worse health care. Older adults may be less subject to the influence of the size of the cohort and may even benefit from a larger cohort (as have the elderly in the United States today, as a result of their increasing political influence).[1] As we commented on the studies reviewed in the preceding section, it will be interesting to see whether Holinger's findings are replicated in the 1980s and 1990s when data become available for this years.

Related to Holinger's research is an earlier study from Lester (1973) exploring the association of the ratio of children under the age of 15 in a nation to those aged 15 to 64 and the ratio of the elderly over the age of 65 to those aged 15 to 64 (the so-called age-dependency ratios) to the suicide and homicide rates of the nations in 1965.

In general, the higher the proportion of children in a nation, the higher the homicide rate and the lower the suicide rate. In contrast, the higher the proportion of elderly in a nation, the lower the homicide rate and the higher the suicide rate.

Lester also explored these associations for each age group. The same results as those above were found for the suicide and homicide rates of those aged 65 to 74 and those 75 and older, that is, the greater the proportion of children in the nation, the lower the suicide rate and the higher the homicide rate of the elderly; whereas the greater the proportion of elderly in the nation, the higher the suicide rate and the lower the homicide rate of the elderly. The homicide rates of youths (aged 15 to 24) in the nations followed the same pattern as the homicide rates of the elderly, but the suicide rates of youths in the nations were not on the whole associated with the age-dependency ratios.

Thus, a higher proportion of children in a society was associated with the externalization of aggression, while a high proportion of elderly was associated with the internalization of aggression. In this study,

---

[1] Research on other suicidal phenomena has indicated that sometimes the smaller the population of the subgroup, the higher the rate of suicide. For example, Lester (1989) noted that the immigrant groups in Australia with fewer members had higher suicide rates. Clearly, such a "social deviancy" theory cannot explain Holinger's results.

however, Lester failed to control for the strong associations between the level of economic development in a nation and the rates of personal violence.

Short-Term Impacts

As Phillips (1989) has noted, suicide can be studied both as a chronic and as an acute process. The impact of the social variables in the research discussed above is a chronic process with the interaction between the independent variable (social conditions) and the dependent variable (suicide) taking place over many months or years. In contrast, research on a topic such as the influence of television news stories about suicide on the suicide rate in the following few days fits better into the perspective of suicide as an acute process.

There has been little research on variables that might have a short-term impact on the suicide rates of younger and older adults. However, Stack (1991), in an examination of the impact of television news stories about suicide on suicide rates, found that news stories of young suicides had a significant impact on the suicide rate of the young (aged 15 to 34 years) in the month of the story. The same phenomenon was found for persons over 65 years of age in reaction to news stories about elderly suicides, but no effect was found for adults aged 35 to 64.

Discussion

All too often, studies of suicide in subgroups of the population, whether it be the elderly, Native Americans, alcoholics, or some other group of interest, fail to identify correlates and determinants of suicide in these groups that differ from those found in general. For example, Bock and Webber (1972) found that the suicide rate of the elderly was higher among those who were more socially isolated. This finding is true for suicides in general and has no special importance for the elderly. In this review of the research conducted on social and economic correlates of the suicide rate of the elderly, therefore, it is important to distinguish between results found for suicide in general and those found for the elderly in particular.

Regional studies identified very few differences in the social correlates of the suicide rate of the young and of the elderly. This is quite surprising, since the social conditions of the elderly are quite different from those of the young. As Stack (1991) noted, the elderly encounter many stressful life events that are uncommon for younger adults, such as death of a spouse, social isolation, and physical illness. Retirement, in particular, and the resulting change in life style is a stressor restricted to the elderly adult.

Financial pressures are also common for the elderly living on fixed incomes that may not be sufficient to meet their needs. In line with this, Yang's (1990) time-series research on U.S. suicide rates found that the suicide rate of the elderly was more responsive to general economic conditions (as measured by the gross national product per capita) than to social conditions. Within the elderly, though, the suicide rate of older women was a little more responsive to social conditions than the suicide rate of older men and the suicide rate of older nonwhites more responsive to social conditions than the suicide rate of older whites.

It is of interest that the results of the time-series studies of the elderly suicide rate are not completely consistent with the results of the regional studies, raising the general issue of whether different sociological theories are required to account for time-series and for regional effects. Future sociological research must explore this issue further.

The present results are pertinent to an important issue raised recently by Moksony (1990) and Taylor (1990), who both argued that many sociological studies of suicide have focused on the relationship between one or two social indicators and the social suicide rate. For example, suicide rates are generally found to be higher when and where divorce rates are higher, as we have seen above. This sociological finding has a parallel at the individual level, for divorced people are found to have higher suicide rates than single or married individuals (Danigelis & Pope, 1979).

Moksony and Taylor noted that the association between divorce and suicide, for example, is not as simple as it seems. Suicide rates in societies where divorce is common are higher, not only in those who are divorced, but also in those who are single or married. They suggested that divorce is an indicator of some more-basic societal quality, and it is this societal quality that is associated with suicidal behavior. Durkheim (1897), of course, proposed two societal qualities, namely social integration and social regulation.

The present review has identified results consistent with this view. For example, in Lester's (1991) factor-analytic study of American states, the suicide rate of the elderly was found to be associated with scores on a general factor (that is, a cluster of variables) with loadings from high divorce rates, high interstate migration rates, low rates of church attendance, and heavier alcohol consumption—a measure of some societal characteristic of the regions as a whole, a quality Lester labelled "social disintegration."

It is important to note that the social indicators in much of the research reviewed were in general measured for the societal populations overall and not for the elderly in those states. Thus, the divorce rate represented everyone in the state rather than the elderly alone. We found fewer studies that had explored the association between the suicide rates of different age groups, either over time or over region, with the social characteristics of those different age groups, except for the studies by Holinger and by Pescosolido and Wright.

Our conclusion is, therefore, that we have not yet moved far enough in identifying *unique* correlates of the regional variation and temporal variation in the elderly suicide rate of a society. As a result, it is difficult at present to propose unique determinants of the suicide rate of the elderly in a society from a sociological perspective. However, we can conclude that, at the regional level of analysis, divorce does not seem to have detrimental impact on the suicide rate of the elderly, while, over time, economic prosperity does seem to have a beneficial impact.

However, some of the social variables studied in the research reviewed, such as social isolation and divorce, occur with different frequencies in the elderly than in younger adults. Those variables may, therefore, have great importance for estimating the suicidal risk of the elderly.

References

Bock, E., & Webber, I. (1972). Social status and relational system of elderly suicide. *Life-Threatening Behavior, 2,* 145–159.

Danigelis, N., & Pope, W. (1979). Durkheim's theory of suicide as applied to the family. *Social Forces, 57,* 1081–1106.

Durkheim, E. (1897). *Le suicide.* Paris: Felix Alcan.

Easterlin, R. A. (1980). *Birth and fortune.* New York: Basic Books.

Holinger, P. C. (1987). *Violent deaths in the United States.* New York: Guilford.

Holinger, P. C., & Lester, D. (1991). Suicide, homicide, and demographic shifts. *Journal of Nervous & Mental Disease, 179,* 574–575.

Lester, D. (1973). Suicide, homicide, and age dependency ratios. *International Journal of Aging & Human Development, 4,* 127–132.

Lester, D. (1983). Preventive effect of strict handgun control laws on suicide rates. *American Journal of Psychiatry, 140,* 1259.

Lester, D. (1984). *Gun control: Issues and answers.* Springfield, IL: Charles Thomas.

Lester, D. (1987). The stability of national suicide rates in Europe. *Sociology & Social Research, 71,* 208.

Lester, D. (1988a). Youth suicide: A cross-cultural perspective. *Adolescence, 23,* 955–958.

Lester, D. (1988b). A regional analysis of suicide and homicide rates in the USA. *Social Psychiatry & Psychiatric Epidemiology, 23,* 202–205.

Lester, D. (1989). *Suicide from a sociological perspective.* Springfield, IL: Charles Thomas.

Lester, D. (1991). Social correlates of youth suicide rates in the United States. *Adolescence, 26,* 55–58.

Moksony, F. (1990). Ecological analysis of suicide. In D. Lester (Ed.), *Current concepts of suicide* (pp. 121–138). Philadelphia: Charles Press.

Pescolsolido, B. A., & Wright, E. R. (1990). Suicide and the role of the family over the life course. *Family Perspective, 24*, 41–58.

Phillips, D. P. (1989). Recent advances in suicidology. In R. F. W. Diekstra, R. Maris, S. Platt, A. Schmidtke, & G. Sonneck (Eds.), *Suicide and its prevention* (pp. 299–312). Leiden: E. J. Brill.

Stack, S. (1981). Suicide and religion. *Sociological Focus, 14*, 207–220.

Stack, S. (1991). Social correlates of suicide by age. In A. A. Leenaars (Ed.), *Life span perspectives of suicide* (pp. 187–213). New York: Plenum.

Taylor, S. (1990). Suicide, Durkheim, and sociology. In D. Lester (Ed.), *Current concepts of suicide* (pp. 225–236). Philadelphia: Charles Press.

Yang, B. (1990, March). *The impact of the economy on suicide in different social and demographic groups.* Presented at the Eastern Economic Association, Cincinnati, OH.

4

Biology of Elderly Suicide

A. H. Rifai, MD, C. F. Reynolds, MD, and J. J. Mann, MD
Western Psychiatric Institute and Clinic, University of Pittsburgh School of Medicine

ABSTRACT: Most studies of suicide in younger patients have demonstrated significant alterations in the serotonin system. Although a high percentage of completed suicides occur in late-life, to date very few studies of the biology of suicide have focused on this age group. This chapter describes age-related changes in the central nervous system pertinent to the biology of suicide, then reviews port-mortem biological studies of the brains of suicides and suicide attempters. As suicide attempts in the elderly are characterized by the use of violent means, biologic studies of impulsive violence are discussed. Finally we describe data on the effect of degenerative diseases on the serotonin system and the possible link to increased suicidal behavior in affected patients. This review underscores the need for further study of the biology of suicide in the geriatric age group.

The traditional view of suicide as an end-point of depressive pathology has been challenged by the high incidence of suicide associated with schizophrenia (Johns, Stanley, & Stanley, 1986), personality disorders (Miles, 1977), and other disorders in the absence of depression (e.g., panic disorder; see Weissmann, Klerman, & Markowitz, 1989). Accordingly, recent studies of suicide have focused on identifying clinical and biological differences between suicide attempters and nonattempters within the same diagnostic categories. This strategy allows the identification of correlates of suicidal behavior within a specific diagnostic group.

In the past two decades, biological studies of suicide have identified several areas of research:

The authors wish to thank Benoit H. Mulsant, MD, for his review of the manuscript. Connie Johnston provided expert secretarial assistance.

This work was supported in part by PHS Grant No. MH-46745.

Address correspondence to A. Hind Rifai, MD, Room 1234, Western Psychiatric Institute & Clinic, 3811 O'Hara Street, Pittsburgh, PA 15213.

1. A search for biologic markers of suicidality that could be used clinically for more accurate risk prediction and thereby prevention.
2. Development of an explanatory model of suicidal behavior that incorporates neurobiology.
3. Defining separately a genetic predisposition to suicide (trait) and illness induced or stress-induced biological predispositions (state-dependent).
4. The relationship of the biology of suicide to the biology of aggressive behavior.

The finding of a genetic risk factor for suicide (Lester, 1986) suggests that there may be detectible biologic markers. Among the neurotransmitter systems implicated in the pathology of suicide, the serotonergic system appears to play a central role: Most studies of the biology of suicidal behavior in vivo and post-mortem have implicated aspects of its functioning (Van Praag, 1982). However, only a few of the numerous published studies of the biology of suicide have included the elderly (60 years of age and over) among their subjects, and very few to date have studied this population exclusively. As in other fields of aging research, difficulties in establishing aging norms and effects of aging make it difficult to extrapolate from results of studies in midlife adults. Moreover, the sharp increase in suicide rates in people over 70 years of age (Fredericks, 1978; Murphy & Wetzel, 1980) suggests that additional or novel processes may become operative.

This review first briefly describes normal aging effects on brain monoamine systems (focusing on the serotonergic system), then describes the biological studies of suicide attempters and completers.

Normal Aging and Biogenic Amines

Data regarding changes occurring in the normal aging brain are scarce. However, there is strong evidence (Carlsson, Adolfsson, Aquilonius, Gottfries, Oreland, Svennerholm, & Winblad, 1980) supporting the existence of *generalized* age-related *atrophy* that is more pronounced in the temporal, frontal, and parietal lobes, and *localized neuronal loss* affecting certain brain regions, for example, the locus ceruleus and substantia nigra (Carlsson et al., 1980).

Likewise, changes in neurotransmitter levels and enzyme activity vary among different brain areas. Post-mortem studies have demonstrated age-related *decreases* in the levels of: dopamine in the nigrostriatal system, norepinephrine in the hippocampus and locus ceruleus, and serotonin (5-hydroxytryptamine [5-HT]) in the cingulate gyrus, but an *increase* of 5-HT in the medulla oblongata (Samorajski, 1977).

Some investigators have reported a positive correlation between age and monoamine metabolites in the cerebrospinal fluid (CSF) (Banki & Molnar, 1981). Other factors, such as decreased transport across the arachnoid villi and CSF turnover, might affect the level of these metabolites in normal controls (Pare, Yeng, Price, & Stacey, 1969).

There is agreement on a generalized age-related decline in most biogenic amine enzyme systems, more pronounced in certain brain areas, with the notable exception of monoamine oxidase-B (MAO-B) which has been found to have age-related increased activity in several brain regions (Fowler, Oreland, Marcusson & Winblad, 1980; Mann, Stanley, McBride, & McEwen, 1986).

Suicidal Behavior and Biogenic Amines

The biologic studies of suicide can be divided into post-mortem studies of the brains of suicide victims and in vivo studies of suicide attempters.

Post-Mortem Studies of Suicide Victims

Serotonergic System
    Neurotransmitter and Metabolite Levels. Multiple studies of suicide brains have found a modest *decrease in serotonin and/or its metabolite 5-hydroxyindolacetic acid (5-HIAA) in the brain stem* (Beskow, Gottfries, Roos, & Windland, 1976; Bourne et al., 1968; Korpi et al., 1986; Lloyd, Farley, Deck, & Horneykiewicz, 1974; Shaw, Camps, & Eccleston, 1967). No reduction of serotonin or 5-HIAA has been confirmed in any other brain regions. Findings specifically pertinent to the elderly (aged 60 years and older) are presented in Table 1. Most of these studies included some older patients, but the number of such patients was too small to permit analysis or conclusions.

    Receptor Studies. The measurement of specific receptors provides information regarding the functional status of neuronal systems prior to death. Receptor studies involving the serotonergic system have investigated multiple receptor subtypes.

The presynaptic serotonin transporter site (imipramine binding site, [^{3}H] IMI) is located on serotonergic nerve terminals and is involved in serotonin reuptake; it can be quantified by its ability to bind ligands such as tritiated imipramine or paroxetine. Several, but not all, studies have demonstrated a significant decrease in the number of binding sites in brains of suicides versus controls (Crow et al., 1984; Perry, Marshall, Blessed, Tomlinson, & Perry, 1983; Stanley, Virgilio, & Gershon, 1982). Gross-Isseroff, Israeli, and Biegon (1989), in a study including older patients (overall age range 21 to 72 years), failed to replicate the finding of decreased [^{3}H] IMI sites in the prefrontal cortex but showed decreases, increases, or no change in other brain regions. The study confirmed previous findings of a positive correlation between binding and age (Owen et al., 1986), most significantly in the basal ganglia and temporal cortex.

The 5-HT$_2$ receptor is a postsynaptic serotonin receptor partially regulated by the concentration of serotonin in the synaptic space. Studies of this receptor in the brain of suicides have shown an increase in 5-HT$_2$ receptors (Arango, 1990; Cheetham, Crompton, Katona, & Horton, 1988; Stanley & Mann, 1983). This effect is more pronounced in the prefrontal cortex than in the temporal pole.

The 5-HT$_1$ receptor has been less extensively studied. Data from limited studies suggest that the number of these receptors is unaltered in suicide victims (Mann et al., 1986). These studies need to be redone, because several subtypes of 5-HT$_1$ receptors have now been identified.

Enzyme System Alterations. MAO-B is the principal serotonin catabolic enzyme. MAO activity had been found to be reduced in the brain of alcoholic suicides in post-mortem studies (Gottfries, Oreland, Wiberg, & Winblad, 1975). Only two patients and eight controls aged 60 years or older were included in the study. More recent studies in nonalcoholic suicides did not find any differences in MAO-A or -B enzyme kinetics compared to nonsuicide control (Mann & Stanley, 1984).

Noradrenergic System

Preliminary data have shown an increase in beta-adrenergic binding in the prefrontal cortex of suicide victims (Mann et al., 1986).

In one study (Biegon & Israeli, 1988), three patients over 60 years of age were included. No significant effect of age was found on beta-adrenergic receptor density.

Ferrier et al. (1986) reported a statistically nonsignificant increase in alpha$_1$-adrenergic receptors in the brain of elderly major depressive nonsuicides (mean age = 75 ± 6 years). Beta-adrenergic receptors were unchanged.

GABA-ergic System

The GABA-ergic system has been implicated in the etiology of anxiety and the mechanism of action of the benzodiazepines. The frequent presentation of anxiety in depressed elderly makes this area of investigation important.

Manchon et al. (1987), in a study of suicides ranging in age from 20 to 78 years, reported an increase in benzodiazepine binding in the

TABLE 1. Post-Mortem Studies

Reference	Biologic Amine Concentration	Sample and Number of Patients		Age (Years)	Elderly Patients	Findings	Findings Relevant for Late-Life
Shaw et al., 1967	5-HT in hind brain	Death from suicide vs. Death physical illness	28 17	Undetermined	5 controls >65 3 patients 60–65	5-HT level in hind brains of depressed patients lower than control 205 mg/g vs. 307 mg/g p < 0.05	No influence of age found
Bourne et al., 1968	5-HT, 5-HIAA, NA in hind brain	Depressed suicides Nondepressed suicides Control	16 7 28	23–71 17–66 29–86	5 > 62 one 66 11 > 62	5-HT NA no difference 5-HIAA lower in hind brain of suicides	
Pare et al., 1969	5-HT, NA, DA in brain stem, hypothalmus and caudate	Suicide by gas coal Control	26 15	Mean age 49 63	12 > 50 mean age 63 ± 3	No difference in 5-HIAA, NA, DA 5-HT decreased in suicides	Positive correlation between age and 5-HT concentrations in controls only

Study	Measure	Group	N	Age	Notes	Results
Cochran et al., 1975	5-HT, in 33 areas of brain	Depressed suicides Alcoholic suicides Control	10 9 12	36–79 32–53 33–74	3 0 4	No differences among diagnostic groups in any areas studied
Lloyd et al., 1976	5-HT, 5-HIAA in brain stem	Suicides Control	5 5	39–51 56–77	Undetermined	Lower brain stem: decreased 5-HT, normal 5-HIAA. Higher brain stem: normal 5-HT, increased 5-HIAA
Ferrier et al., 1986	5-HIAA in frontal cortex	MAD Dysthymic Control	9 7 6	75 ± 6 81 ± 5 76 ± 6	All patients are elderly	No differences in the 3 groups. Trends towards lower 5-HIAA levels in MAD patients.

MAD = Major Affective Disorder
5-HT = 5-Hydroxytryptamine
5-HIAA = 5-Hydroxyindoleacetic Acid
NA = Noradrenaline

hippocampus. This finding was replicated in a study involving younger patients (Cheetham et al., 1987).

Summary

Although considerable data implicate the serotonergic and possibly also the adrenergic and GABA-ergic systems in suicide, no specific relevant data are available in the elderly with the exception of a negative study in depressive nonsuicides (Ferrier et al., 1986).

In-Vivo Studies of Suicide Attempters

Three major approaches have been employed to study biological correlates of suicidal behavior in patients identified as being at high risk (e.g., past or recent attempters): (1) measurement of neurotransmitter metabolite levels in the CSF prospectively or after an attempt, (2) neuroendocrine challenge tests, and (3) blood platelet studies.

Studies of CSF 5-HIAA

In a landmark study, Åsberg, Thorén, Träskman, Bertilsson, and Ringberger (1976) reported that CSF levels of 5-HIAA were bimodally distributed in depressed patients, and that the patients with low 5-HIAA levels had a higher rate of suicide attempts. Subsequently, they found that patients in this low CSF 5-HIAA group were at a significantly increased risk of completed suicide within 12 months compared to patients with normal levels of CSF 5-HIAA (Träskman, Åsberg, Bertilsson, & Sjöstrand, 1981).

This finding has been replicated by other investigators in multiple studies of patients suffering from unipolar depression (López-Ibor, Saiz-Ruiz, & Pérez de los Cobos, 1985), schizophrenia (van Praag, 1983), and personality disorders (Brown et al., 1982), but not from bipolar disorder (Roy-Byrne, Post, & Rubinow, 1983). Studies including elderly patients are listed in Table 2. Only Jones et al. (1990) focused on the elderly and confirmed the presence of low CSF 5-HIAA and HVA in older suicide attempters compared to nonattempters.

In general studies of CSF, HVA or 3-methoxy-4-hydroxyphenylglycol (MHPG) have yielded less consistent results than studies of CSF 5-HIAA. Other CSF studies including CSF corticotropin releasing hormone (CRH), cortisol, adrenocorticotrophic hormone (ACTH), and magnesium and calcium ions (Banki, Arató, & Kilts, 1986) are still preliminary and none have focused on the elderly.

Neuroendocrine Studies of Serotonergic Function

Several agents have been used to test the functional responsivity of the serotonergic system in suicide attempters. The prolactin response to an acute challenge with fenfluramine (an indirect serotonin agonist) is a good overall index of serotonergic activity. It assesses both transmitter availability and receptor sensitivity.

TABLE 2. CSF Studies

Reference	Biologic Amine Concentration	Sample and Number of Patients	Age (Years) Mean ± SD	Elderly Patients	Findings	Findings Relevant for Late-Life
Jones et al., 1990	CSF HIAA, HVA	Depressed after suicide attempt 12 Depressed with no suicide attempt 9 vs. Controls 7	63.2 (6.8) 64.7 (7.3) 71.3 (6.7)	All	Suicide attempters had significantly lower concentrations of both CSF 5-HIAA and HVA	Mean (SD) HIAA ng/ml HVA ng/ml 19 (7) 30 ± 14 26 ± 7 49 ± 21 26 ± 4 45 ± 16
Banki et al., 1984	CSF 5-HIAA, HVA	Sample: Total 141 pts. Females MAD Schizophrenia Alcoholics Adjustment Disorder 52 Suicide Attempters	21–71	Undetermined	CSF 5-HIAA Significantly lower in violent attempters in all categories	
Träskman et al., 1981	CSF 5-HIAA, HVA, MHPG	Psychiatric patients 30 Healthy volunteers 45	21–65	1 pt. –65	*Short-Term* 1. Decreased 5-HIAA in suicidal pts. *Long-Term* 2. Predictor of future completed suicides 20% within 1 year	
Asberg et al., 1976	CSF 5-HIAA	Depressed patients (endogenous and reactive) 68	23–88	4 pts.	-CSF 5-HIAA has bimodal distributions -Low CSF 5-HIAA indicator of future suicide	

HVA = Homovanillic Acid
MHPG = 3-Methoxy-4-Hydroxyphenylglycol

Coccaro et al. (1989) demonstrated a blunted prolactin response in suicide attempters (mean age = 46 ± 13 years), irrespective of the length of time elapsed since the most recent suicide attempt. Thus, this finding may represent a lifetime biologic characteristic of these patients (trait rather than state). We have reported that peak prolactin values are significantly correlated with age and show a significant decrease by approximately 30 years of age (McBride, Tierney, DeMeo, Chen, & Mann, 1990). From age 30 through midlife, there is little change in the prolactin response to fenfluramine. No data are available in the elderly. An association was also found between the blunted prolactin response and measures of aggressivity and impulsivity in nondepressed patients (Coccaro et al., 1989).

Platelet Studies in Suicide Attempters

Blood platelets contain components of the serotonergic system. Because of their availability, they are studied as "proxies" of the central nervous system (Oreland et al., 1981). A variety of platelet serotonergic measures have been investigated in suicide attempters, including platelet serotonin content, MAO-B activity, 5-HT uptake kinetics, [^{3}H] imipramine binding, and 5-HT$_2$ receptor binding. No significant association has been found between suicidal behavior and platelet serotonin content, MAO activity, 5-HT uptake or imipramine binding (Meltzer & Airoa 1986).

Pandey, Pandey, Janicak, Marks, and Davis (1990) reported increased platelet 5-HT$_2$ binding in depressed suicide attempters compared to nonattempters, but they found no significant effect of age on binding.

Other Studies

Sleep Studies and Suicide. Recent data linking sleep biology to the serotonin system have increased interest in the investigation of sleep alterations in suicide attempters. Serotonin is thought to regulate REM sleep activity. Hypofunction of the serotonergic system, as in suicidal patients or in depression, may result in REM sleep disorganization. A study of the sleep EEG of adult depressives (Sabo, Reynolds, Kupfer, Berman, & March, 1991) found that suicide attempters had longer sleep latency, lower sleep efficiency, and altered intranight distribution of phasic REM activity with increased REM activity in REM period 2.

A similar study by our laboratory in a small sample of elderly depressives revealed a statistically significant decrease in sleep efficiency and total time spent asleep in suicide attempters compared with nonattempters (Reynolds et al., unpublished data, 1991).

Studies of Violence and Suicide

Suicide has been viewed by psychodynamic theorists as a form of internally directed aggression. Thus, biological studies of aggression and impulsivity are considered relevant to the biology of suicide. Relatively low levels of CSF 5-HIAA have been found in impulsive violent offenders against person and property (Brown, Goodwin, Ballenger, Goyer, & Major, 1979; Brown et al., 1982). One of these studies demonstrated that impulsive violent offenders with a history of suicide attempts had the lowest CSF 5-HIAA levels (Linnoila et al., 1983).

Banki and Arató (1983) reported low CSF 5-HIAA in a group of depressed patients who used violent methods in their suicide attempt, but failed to find a similar association in the patients who attempted suicide by tranquillizer overdose.

CSF 5-HIAA has thus been postulated to be a marker for impulsive aggression. No comparable data are available in the elderly, for whom externally directed violence is uncommon but suicide attempts are characterized by a high degree of premeditation and the use of violent methods (Frierson, 1991).

Suicide in Brain Degenerative Illnesses

Recent investigations have focused on the effect of degenerative brain changes on the serotonin system and the possible biologic predisposition to suicide in patients with degenerative dementia (Cross & Crow, 1984).

Despite reports of increased rates of suicide in dementia and organic brain syndromes (Murphy, 1986), no definitive data are available at this time regarding possible increased rates of suicide in patients with Alzheimer's disease.

Cross et al. (1984) conducted post-mortem studies of patients aged 70 years and older with senile dementia of the Alzheimer type. They found evidence of degeneration of noradrenergic and serotonergic innervation of the cerebral cortex with loss of serotonin $5-HT_1$ and $5-HT_2$ receptors, particularly in the temporal lobe. They also found a decrease in imipramine binding in subjects with a history of depression who had committed suicide. No consistent changes were found in monoamine metabolites.

In Huntington's disease (HD), rates of suicide are significantly elevated when compared to rates in the age- and gender-matched general population (Caine & Shoulson, 1983; Shoulson, 1986). Kurlan, Caine, Rubin, and Nemeroff (1988) studied CSF metabolites from 56 HD patients with major depression (mean age $= 39 \pm 10$ years). They found no difference in CSF 5-HIAA concentrations between patients and normal controls. This sample represents an early age of onset of HD, in which psychiatric manifestations (personality changes, depression and suicidal ideations) dominate the clinical picture prior to the emergence of dementia and neurologic deficits.

Summary

Various biologic parameters, primarily related to the serotonergic system, have been found to correlate with suicidal behavior. Most studies have not included a meaningful number of subjects over 60 years of age. Given the significant effects of normal aging on many of these systems, it would be hazardous to extrapolate from findings in younger and midlife adults to the elderly. Studies are urgently needed in this age group where organicity and senescence coincide with a pronounced increase in rates of completed suicides.

References

Ågren, H. (1980). Symptom patterns in unipolar and bipolar depression correlating with monoamine metabolites in the cerebrospinal fluid: II. Suicide. *Psychiatry Research, 3*, 225–236.

Arango, V., Ernsberger, P., Marzuk, P. M., Chen, J. S., Tierney, H., Stanley, M., Reis, D. J., & Mann, J. J. (1990, Nov.). Autoradiographic demonstration of increased serotonin 5-HT$_2$ and beta-adrenergic receptor binding sites in the brain of suicide victims. *Archives of General Psychiatry, 47*(11), 1038–1047.

Åsberg, M., Thorén, P., Träskman, L., Bertilsson, L., & Ringberger, V. (1976). Serotonin depression—a biochemical subgroup within the affective disorders. *Science, 191*, 470–480.

Banki, C. M., & Arató, M. (1983). Amine metabolites and neuroendocrine responses related to depression and suicide. *Journal of Affective Disorders, 5*, 223–232.

Banki, C. M., Arató, M., & Kilts, C. D. (1986). Aminergic studies and cerebrospinal fluid cations in suicide. *Annals of New York Academy of Sciences, 487*, 221–230.

Banki, C. M., Arató, M., Papp, Z., & Kurcz, M. (1984). Biochemical markers in suicidal patients. Investigations with cerebrospinal fluid amine metabolites and neuroendocrine tests. *Journal of Affective Disorders, 6*, 341–350.

Banki, C. M., & Molnar, G. (1981). The influence of age, height, and body weight on cerebrospinal fluid amine metabolites and tryptophan in women. *Biological Psychiatry, 16*, 753–762.

Beskow, J., Gottfries, C. G., Roos, B. E., & Windland, B. (1976). Determination of monoamine and monoamine metabolites in the human brain: Postmortem studies in a group of suicides and in a control group. *Acta Psychiatrica Scandinavia, 53*, 7–20.

Biegon, A., & Israeli, M. (1988). Regionally selective increases in β-adrenergic receptor density in the brains of suicide victims. *Brain Research, 442*, 199–203.

Bourne, H. R., Bunney, W. E., Colburn, R. W., Davis, J. M., Shaw, D. M., & Coppen, A. J. (1968). Noradrenaline, 5-hydroxytryptamine, and 5-hydroxyindoleacetic acid in hindbrains of suicidal patients. *The Lancet, 2*, 805–808.

Brown, G. L., Goodwin, F. K., Ballenger, J. C., Goyer, P. F., & Major, L. F. (1979). Aggression in human correlates with cerebrospinal fluid amine metabolites. *Psychiatry Research, 1*, 131–139.

Brown, G. L., Ebert, M., Goyer, P. F., Jimersom, D. C., Klein, W. J., Bunney, W. E., & Goodwin, F. K. (1982). Aggression, suicide and serotonin: Relationships to CSF amine metabolites. *American Journal of Psychiatry, 139*, 741–746.

Caine, E. D., & Shoulson, I. (1983). Psychiatric syndromes in Huntington's disease. *American Journal of Psychiatry, 140*, 728–733.

Carlsson, A., Adolfsson, R., Aquilonius, S. M., Gottfries, C. G., Oreland, L., Svennerholm, L., & Winblad, B. (1980). Biogenic amines in human brain in normal aging, senile dementia, and chronic alcoholism. In M. Goldstein (Ed.), *Ergot compounds and brain function: Neuropsychiatric aspects* (pp. 295–304). New York: Raven Press.

Cheetham, S. C., Crompton, M. R., Katona, C. L. E., Horton, R. W., Parker, S. J., & Reynolds, G. B. (1987, April). GABA$_A$ and benzodiazepine binding sites in the cortex of depressed suicide victims. *International Conference on New Directions in Affective Disorders* (Abstract No. N532), Jerusalem.

Cheetham, S. C., Crompton, M. R., Katona, C. L. E., & Horton, R. W. (1988). Brain 5-HT$_2$ receptor binding sites in depressed suicide victims. *Brain Research, 443*, 272–280.

Coccaro, E. F., Siever, J. J., Klar, H. M., Maurer, G., Cochrane, K., Cooper, T. B., Mohs, R. C., & Davis, K. L. (1989). Serotonergic studies in patients with affective and personality disorders. *Archives of General Psychiatry, 46*, 587–599.

Cochran, E., Robins, E., & Grote, S. (1976). Regional serotonin levels in brain: A comparison of depressive suicides and alcoholic suicides with controls. *Biological Psychiatry, 11*, 283–294.

Cross, A. J., Crow, T. J., Ferrier, I. N., Johnson, J. A., Bloom, S. R., & Corsellis, J. A. N. (1984, Dec.). Serotonin receptor changes in dementia of the Alzheimer type. *Journal of Neurochemistry, 43*(6), 1574–1581.

Crow, T. J., Cross, A. J., Cooper, S. J., Deakin, J. F. W., Ferrier, I. N., Johnson, J. A., Joseph, M. H., Owen, F., Poulter, M., Lofthouse, R., Corsellis, J. A. N., Chambers, D. R., Blessed, G., Perry, E. K., Perry, R. H., & Tomlinson, B. E. (1984). Neurotransmitter receptors and monoamine metabolites in the brains of patients with Alzheimer-type dementia and depression, and suicides. *Neuropharmacology, 23*, 1561–1569.

Ferrier, I. N., McKeith, I. G., Cross, A. J., Perry, E. K., Candy, J. M., & Perry, R. H. (1986). Postmortem neurochemical studies in depression: Psychobiology of suicidal behavior. *Annals of New York Academy of Sciences, 487*, 128–142.

Fredericks, C. (1978). Current trends in suicidal behavior in the United States. *American Journal of Psychotherapy, 32*, 172–201.

Fowler, C. J., Oreland, L., Marcusson, J., & Winblad, B. (1980, April). Titration of human brain monoamine oxidase-A and -B by clorgyline and L-reprenil. *Archives of Pharmacology, 311*(3), 263–272.

Frierson, R. L. (1991). Suicide attempts by the old and the very old. *Archives of Internal Medicine, 151*, 141–144.

Gottfries, C. G., Oreland, L., Wiberg, A., & Winblad, B. (1975). Lowered monoamine oxidase activity in brains from alcoholic suicides. *Journal of Neurochemistry, 25*, 667–673.

Gross-Isseroff, R., Israeli, M., & Biegon, A. (1989). Autoradiographic analysis of titrated imipramine binding in the human brain postmortem: Effects of suicide. *Archives of General Psychiatry, 46*, 237–241.

Johns, C. A., Stanley, M., & Stanley, B. (1986). Suicide in schizophrenia: Psychobiology of suicidal behavior. *Annals of New York Academy of Sciences, 487*, 294–300.

Jones, J. S., Stanley, B., Mann, J. J., Frances, A. J., Guido, J. R., Traskman-Bendz, L., Winchel, R., Brown, R. P., & Stanley, M. (1990). CSF 5-HIAA and HVA concentrations in elderly depressed patients who attempted suicide. *American Journal of Psychiatry, 147*, 1225–1227.

Kurlan, R., Caine, E., Rubin, A., & Nemeroff, C. (1988). Cerebrospinal fluid correlates of depression in Huntington's disease. *Archives of Neurology, 45*, 881–883.

Korpi, E. R., Kleinman, J., Goodman, S. I., Phillips, I., DeLisi, L. E., Linnoila, M., & Wyatt, R. J. (1986). Serotonin and 5-hydroxyindoleacetic acid in brains of suicide victims. *Archives of General Psychiatry, 43*, 594–600.

Lester, D. (1986). Genetics, twin studies, and suicide. In R. Maris (Ed.), *Biology of suicide* (pp. 192–203). New York: The Guilford Press.

Linnoila, M., Virkkunen, M., Scheinin, M., Nuutila, A., Rimond, R., & Goodwin, F. K. (1983, Dec.). Low cerebrospinal fluid 5-hydroxyindoleacetic acid concentration differentiates impulsive from non-impulsive violent behavior. *Life Sciences, 33*(26), 2609–2614.

Lloyd, K. G., Farley, I. J., Deck, J. H. N., & Horneykiewicz, O. (1974). Serotonin and 5-hydroxyindoleacetic acid in discrete areas of the brainstem of suicide victims and control patients. In E. Costa, G. L. Gressa, & M. Sandler (Eds.), *Advances in biochemical psychopharmacology* (Vol. 11, pp. 378–397). New York: Raven Press.

López-Ibor, J. J., Saiz-Ruiz, J., & Pérez de los Cobos, J. C. (1985). Biological correlations of suicide and aggressivity in major depressions (with melancholia): 5-Hydroxyindoleacetic acid and cortisol in cerebral spinal fluid, dexamethasone suppression test and therapeutic response to 5-Hydroxytryptophan. *Neuropsychobiology, 14,* 67–74.

Manchon, M., Kopp, N., Rouzioux, J. J., Lecestre, D., Deluermoz, S., & Maichon, S. (1987). Benzodiazepine receptor and neurotransmitter studies in the brain of suicides. *Life Sciences, 41,* 2623–2630.

Mann, J. J., & Stanley, M. (1984). Postmortem monoamine oxidase enzyme kinetics in the frontal cortex of suicide victims and controls. *Acta Psychiatrica Scandinavia, 69,* 135–139.

Mann, J. J., Stanley, M., McBride, P. A., & McEwen, B. S. (1986). Increased serotonin$_2$ and β-adrenergic receptor binding in the frontal cortices of suicide victims. *Archives of General Psychiatry, 43,* 954–959.

McBride, P. A., Tierney, H., DeMeo, M., Chen, J. S., & Mann, J. J. (1990). Effects of age and gender on CNS serotonergic responsivity in normal adults. *Biological Psychiatry, 27,* 1143–1155.

Meltzer, H. Y., & Airoa, R. C. (1986). Platelets markers of suicidality. Psychobiology of suicidal behavior. *Annals of New York Academy of Sciences, 487,* 271–280.

Miles, C. P. (1977). Conditions predisposing to suicide: A review. *Journal of Nervous and Mental Disease, 164*(4), 231–246.

Murphy, G. E. (1986). Suicide and attempted suicide. In G. Winolur & P. Clayton (Eds.), *The medical basis of psychiatry* (pp. 562–579). Philadelphia: W. B. Saunders.

Murphy, G. E., & Wetzel, R. D. (1980). Suicide risk by birth cohort in the United States, 1949 to 1974. *Archives of General Psychiatry, 37,* 519–523.

Oreland, L., Wiberg, A., Åsberg, M., Träskman, L., Sjöstrand, L., Thorén, P., Bertilsson, L., & Tubrina, G. (1981). Platelet monoamine oxidase activity and monoamine metabolites in cerebrospinal fluid in depressed and suicidal patients and in healthy controls. *Psychiatry Research, 4,* 21–29.

Owen, F., Chambers, D. R., Cooper, S. J., Crow, T. J., Johnson, J. A., Lofthouse, R., & Poulter, M. (1986). Serotonergic mechanisms in brains of suicide victims. *Brain Research, 362,* 185–188.

Pandey, G. N., Pandey, S. C., Janicak, P. G., Marks, R. C., & Davis, J. M. (1990). Platelet serotonin-2 receptor binding sites in depression and suicide. *Biological Psychiatry, 28,* 215–222.

Pare, C. M. B., Yeng, D. P. H., Price, K., & Stacey, R. S. (1969). 5-Hydroxytryptamine, noradrenaline, and dopamine in brainstem, hypothalamus, and caudate nucleus of controls and of patients committing suicide by coal-gas poisoning. *The Lancet, 2,* 133–135.

Perry, E. K., Marshall, E. J., Blessed, G., Tomlinson, B. E., & Perry, R. H. (1983). Decreased imipramine binding in the brains of patients with depressive illness. *British Journal of Psychiatry, 142,* 188–192.

Reynolds, C. F. (1991). [Sleep studies in suicide attempters in late-life unipolar depression]. Unpublished raw data.

Roy-Byrne, P., Post, R. M., & Rubinow, D. R. (1983). CSF 5-HIAA and personal and family history of suicide in affectively ill patients: A negative study. *Psychiatry Research, 10,* 263–274.

Sabo, E., Reynolds, C. F., Kupfer, D. J., Berman, S. R. (March 1991). Sleep, depression, and suicide. *Psychiatry Research, 36*(3), 265–277.

Samorajski, T. (1977). Central neurotransmitter substances and aging: A review. *Journal of American Geriatrics Society, 25*(8), 337–345.

Shaw, D. M., Camps, F. E., & Eccleston, E. G. (1967). 5-Hydroxytryptamine in the hindbrain of depressive suicides. *British Journal of Psychiatry, 113,* 1407–1411.

Shoulson, I. (1986). Huntington's disease. In A. K. Ashbury, G. M. McKhann, & W. I. McDonald (Eds.), *Diseases of the nervous system* (Vol. 2, pp. 1258–1267). Philadelphia: W. B. Saunders.

Stanley, M., & Mann, J. J. (1983). Increased serotonin-2 binding sites in frontal cortex of suicide victims. *The Lancet, 1*, 214–216.

Stanley, M., Virgilio, J., & Gershon, S. (1982). Titrated imipramine binding sites are decreased in the frontal cortex of suicides. *Science, 216*, 1337–1339.

Träskman, L., Åsberg, M., Bertilsson, L., & Sjöstrand, L. (1981). Monoamine metabolites in CSF and suicidal behavior. *Archives of General Psychiatry, 38*, 631–636.

van Praag, H. M. (1982). Depression, suicide and the metabolism of serotonin in the brain. *Journal of Affective Disorders, 4*, 275–290.

van Praag, H. M. (1983). CSF 5-HIAA and suicide in non-depressed schizophrenics. *The Lancet, 1*, 977–978.

Weissmann, M. M., Klerman, G. L., & Markowitz, J. S. (1989). Suicidal ideation and suicide attempts in panic disorder and attacks. *New England Journal of Medicine, 321*, 1209–1214.

5

Suicide Notes of the Older Adult

Antoon A. Leenaars, PhD, C Psych
Windsor, Ontario

ABSTRACT: Although not true in all countries, older adults are the developmental age group at highest risk for death by suicide in the United States. Our knowledge of suicide in the elderly is, however, limited. The psychological characteristics for suicide cannot be attributed primarily or even solely to being old. One avenue to understanding this complicated act in the elderly is suicide notes. Despite their limitations, suicide notes contain special revelations of the human mind and there is much one can learn from them about suicide in the older adult. This paper outlines the sparse literature on the topic of suicide notes of the older adult and then presents the author's own life-span research related to the elderly. The research indicated that long-term instability was critical in understanding suicide in the older adult. However, indirect expressions (e.g., ambivalence, unconscious implications) were much less frequently observed in the notes of the elderly than other adults. The research also found that older males often wrote about painful problems in their interpersonal relations in their final letters and this pain was significant in making their final decision. Future research, specifically regarding a *protocol analysis* based on a review of the research on suicide in the elderly, will be discussed.

In recent years, a great deal of attention has been focused on suicide in the young. However, it is the elderly that are at the highest risk for death by suicide in many countries. I do not wish to imply that the suicide in the young is not tragic, because life expectancy is then the

The author acknowledges the cooperation and assistance of J. Callahan, J. McIntosh, E. Shneidman, J. Richman, and the Department of Psychiatry at the University of Michigan.

Statistics for this paper were compiled by J. Calahan, University of Michigan, and J. McIntosh, Indiana University of South Bend.

The data and tabulations utilized in this publication were made available by the Inter-university Consortium for Political and Social Research. The data for Mortality Detail Files, 1979–1980 (Volume II), 1981–1982 (Volume III), 1983–1984 (Volume IV), 1985 (Volume V), and 1986–1987 (Volume VI) were originally collected and prepared by the National Center for Health Statistics. Neither the collector of the original data nor the Consortium bears any responsibility for the analysis or interpretations presented here.

greatest, since one is then only at the beginning of one's possible life span. Yet, suicide in the elderly, I believe, is equally tragic and can indeed be often prevented.

A difficult problem in suicide is the matter of obtaining suitable data. Shneidman and Farberow (1957), Maris (1981), and others have suggested the following possible data sources: statistics, third party interviews, the study of nonfatal suicide attempters and documents (including suicide notes). Each of these sources has its limitations, yet each has proven valuable in expanding our understanding of suicide. Although there is considerable controversy surrounding the admissibility of personal accounts both historically (Windelband, 1904) and currently (Runyan, 1982), Allport (1942) demonstrated that personal documents have a significant place in social science research. Suicide notes can be an especially rewarding scientific source of data. For example, with respect to life span issues, the very earliest research on suicide notes (Farberow & Shneidman, 1957) clearly indicated that age is important in understanding suicide.

Though published studies on age as a significant variable in the writings of individuals who killed themselves date from Farberow and Shneidman's work, few subsequent studies of suicide notes have examined this variable. The few studies published on age (Darbonne, 1969; Leenaars, 1987, 1988a, 1988b, 1991a; Leenaars & Balance, 1984a; Lester & Hummel, 1980; Lester & Reeve, 1982; Tuckman, Kleiner, & Lavell, 1959) indicate that suicidal characteristics vary with age. Some of this research indeed shows the following: Suicide in older adults is different in some ways from other adults. One observation of concern in the research is the fact that older adults in their notes exhibit a greater wish to die than other adults.

Classification of Age: A Developmental Schema

Various students of suicide notes have divided their age samples differently; this makes direct comparison among studies difficult. Various definitions of young, old, and so on cloud the literature. This problem reflects in part the difficulty of obtaining adequate samples of notes themselves. Given a current archive of over 1,200 suicide notes, I have proposed an *a priori* classification of age in the hope of bringing some clarity into this difficult area (Leenaars, 1987, 1988a). The schema has been influenced by our knowledge of adult development (Colarusso & Nemiroff, 1981; Kalish, 1975; Kimmel, 1974) and by Erikson's theoretical model on the stages (time lines) of such development (Erikson, 1963, 1968). The three groups are young adulthood, middle adulthood, and late adulthood (or older adulthood). The three groups, with characteristics and age ranges, are as follows:

I: Young adulthood (Erikson's stage, intimacy versus isolation; chronological age, 18 to 25);
II: Middle adulthood (Erikson's stage, generativity versus stagnation; chronological age, 25 to 55)
III: Late adulthood (Erikson's stage, integrity versus despair; chronological age, 55 and over)

It is imperative to understand that, from a developmental view, age is not a demographic variable. It is a genotypic view, addressing such questions as "What are the commonalities of a developmental age?" Our schema provides a vector on the study of lives.

I shall recapitulate previous studies here (Leenaars, 1987, 1988a, 1989a, 1989b), hoping to demonstrate how older adults' suicide notes and, by implication, their suicides, are psychologically different from other adults. This observation is important not only to understand the suicides of older adults, but also because most previous studies of suicide notes have utilized Shneidman and Farberow's 1957 sample. The age range for that sample was 25 to 59, being generally consistent with only middle adulthood. We must ask, therefore, if the previously published findings from suicide notes are generalizable across the adult life span and particularly to the elderly. Our understanding of suicide, based on previous studies of suicide notes, may not apply to older adults (or young adults), but to middle adults only.

Suicide by Specified Time Lines

That there are different rates of completed suicide across the life span is a well established fact. Young, middle, and older adults show discretely different rates of suicide in the United States and elsewhere.

A consideration[1] of annual suicide rates by specified age (time line) groups illustrates the different rates of suicide across the adult life span (U.S. Department of Health and Human Services, 1990). Table 1 presents the rates of U.S. suicide by specified age groups from 1980 to 1987. The rates, at least over the eight years (i.e., 1980 to 1987), suggest that adults in late adulthood consistently have the highest suicide rate. Figure 1 presents the same data graphically.

Older adults in the United States have the highest suicide rates of all adults, but the same trend is not evident in other countries such as Canada. In Canada, both young and older adults exhibit high rates

TABLE 1. U.S. Suicides by Specified Age Groups, 1980–1987

Year	18–25 Years Suicide			26–54 Years Suicide			55 Years and up Suicide		
	Pop.	No.	Rate	Pop.	No.	Rate	Pop.	No.	Rate
1980	34,228	5,202	15.20	81,868	12,772	15.60	47,465	7,993	16.84
1981	34,373	5,128	14.92	83,789	13,473	16.08	48,191	8,067	16.74
1982	34,379	5,052	14.70	85,725	13,606	15.87	48,940	8,660	17.70
1983	34,074	4,759	13.97	87,770	13,610	15.51	49,661	8,957	18.04
1984	33,522	4,919	14.67	89,895	13,971	15.54	50,289	9,367	18.63
1985	32,862	4,926	15.00	92,017	13,846	15.05	50,871	9,513	18.70
1986	32,168	4,895	15.22	94,230	14,786	15.69	51,400	10,063	19.58
1987	31,452	4,634	14.73	96,551	14,868	15.40	51,855	10,127	19.53

Note. The population figures are in thousands; the suicide rates are per 100,000.

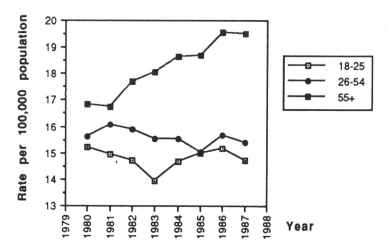

Figure 1.   U.S. suicide rates by specified age groups, 1980–1987.

of suicide across the life span (Health and Welfare, 1987; Leenaars & Lester, 1990). Yet, even if such trends exist elsewhere, the elderly in almost all countries are at considerable risk for death by suicide.

Late Adulthood

Late adulthood is an obvious time-line in development (Frager & Fadiman, 1984; Kimmel, 1974). It is brought upon by one's increasing awareness of personal closeness to death (Kimmel, 1974), and it has its unique psychological issues. There is, however, a consistent controversy regarding what chronological age marks the beginning of this time-line. I tentatively supported the age of 55 (Kimmel, 1974; Neugarten, Moore, & Lowe, 1965), although 60 makes equally reasonable sense. Utilizing the markers of 65 or 70 years makes less sense. These ages appear to be selected more for cultural reasons, such as age of expected retirement, than psychological (developmental) reasons. The age of 65 is also frequently selected in epidemiological studies, because the only available data, such as national statistics for suicide, often make comparisons on 10-year age groupings (i.e., 15 to 24; 25 to 34; etc.) (Lester, 1991; McIntosh, 1991). Of course, no developmental period can be rigidly defined chronologically, and, at best, the marker of 55 approximates what can only be defined developmentally. Some people mature earlier, others later than the mean.

It is important to note that this phase of development has been relatively well charted. It is the final time-line. Late adulthood is a stage marked by the development of a sense of integrity. The older adults continues to develop previous dialectics (such as identity versus identity confusion, intimacy versus isolation, and generativity versus stagnation); however, the crisis of *integrity versus despair* becomes the central issue in the older person's life in Erikson's theoretical perspective.

Erikson (1963, 1968, 1980) was one of the first to pioneer the study of integrity (integrity vs. despair) in late adulthood (although Butler's [1963] concept of life review includes many of the same issues and concerns). By 55 or so, one becomes increasingly aware of the finitude of *one's own* life. Often this is triggered by changes in one's relations to the world, such as decline in health or loss of one's spouse. One begins (although the process might occur to a degree for many throughout the life span) to evaluate one's life: Was my life meaningful? Has it always been unstable? What have I done? Was my life wasted? Was it unbearable? (And etc.)

Erikson (1963) wrote:

It is the ego's accrued assurance of its proclivity for order and meaning. It is a post-narcissistic love of the human ego—not of the self—as an experience which conveys some world order and spiritual sense, no matter how dearly paid for. It is the acceptance of one's one and only life cycle as something that had to be and that, by necessity permitted no substitution. . . . (p. 268)

The acceptance of one's life, one's only life, becomes central. One's whole life is reevaluated; indeed, one's *previous* development plays a crucial role. Has one's life been marked by instability? Have I been intimate? Have I generated something? One's accomplishment, especially one's physical (and mental) offsprings are seen with new meaning. Even one's parents are seen differently. One not only evaluates whether life was meaningful, but whether it was bearable. A positive resolution results in acceptance. A negative resolution results in a deep sense of despair. As Melville noted in *Moby Dick*, those in despair live in "a damp, drizzly November in . . . . (their) . . . . soul."

I do not wish to imply that one's concept of life and death does not develop after 55, only that 55—an arbitrary chronological number—marks the beginning. The person at age 55 or 60 does exhibit an awareness of one's closeness to death; however, such awareness may be different at 70 or 90. Peck (1956) has, in fact, attempted to define the issues of aging more precisely by extending Erikson's insights into greater differentiation. (It would be of interest to study the suicide notes of those aged 55 to 70 and 70 and above—even more refined classifications. This, however, will be work for the future.)

What is *despair*? Erikson (1963) wrote: "Despair expresses the feeling that the time is now short, too short to attempt to start another life, and to try out alternate roads to integrity" (p. 269).

Elsewhere, Erikson (1968) wrote:

Such a despair is often hidden behind a show of disgust, a misanthropy or a chronic contemptuous displeasure with particular institutions and particular people—a disgust and a displeasure which, where not allied with the vision of a superior life, only signifies the individual's contempt of himself. (p. 140)

One's fate is not accepted. One's fellowship is lost. The person's life is meaningless. One's relations (e.g., self, spouse, child, job, book) are meaningless. The individual rejects everything. All was a waste. One plunges into despair. This despair is deep and getting deeper. One *is* despair. And this despair manifests itself in the nonresolution of death; for example, by the fear of death or, in a few, by the invitation to plunge oneself into death.

For most, however, there is a positive resolution and the person develops *wisdom*. Wisdom has many connotations for the older adult, for example, wit, accumulated knowledge, mature judgment, and inclusive understanding. Wisdom develops out of the dialectic of integrity and despair.

Not that each person can evolve wisdom for oneself; for most, the individual's tradition provides the essence. By the end of the life span, those that positively resolve the encounter of integrity and despair develop a sense of wholeness and completeness. One is solid. One accepts oneself (identity) and one's relations (i.e., attachments). Helplessness is alleviated and so is dependence, both being feelings that often mark old age (Frager & Fadiman, 1984). Strength in the old, therefore, "takes the form of wisdom in all of its connotations." Erikson (1964) wrote:

Wisdom, then, is detached concern with life itself, in the face of death itself. It maintains and conveys the integrity of experience, in spite of the decline of bodily and mental functions. It responds to the need of the on-coming generation for an integrated heritage and yet remains aware of the relativity of all knowledge. (p. 133)

Previous Research on Suicide in Older Adults

Research regarding any area of late adulthood has been increasing in the last few decades. Maddox (1987), for example, provides an extensive encyclopedia on topics on aging. Gerontology is now a well-established field. Studies on suicide in this group are, however, too scarce. This lack constituted a reason for developing this volume. Yet, we have learned some basic facts about suicide in the elderly (e.g., Osgood & McIntosh, 1986; Richman, 1991), and I do not wish here to repeat these observations. A few observations, however, may be helpful here:

1. The psychological characteristics for suicide cannot be attributed primarily or even solely to being old (Richman, 1991).

2. Suicide in the elderly is best understood as a multidimensional malaise. Suicide in the older adult is "a conscious act of self-induced annihilation, best understood as a multi-dimensional malaise in a needful individual who defines an issue for which suicide is perceived as the best solution" (Shneidman, 1985, p. 203).

3. There are enormous psychological commonalities of suicide in the elderly and other adults. Understanding suicide through such characteristics as unbearable pain, interpersonal relations, rejection–aggression, inability to adjust, indirect expressions, identification–egression, ego, and cognitive constriction can be most constructive across the life span, including the elderly (Leenaars, 1989b, 1991c).

4. Despite the commonalities, it is useful to understand suicide in the older adult from a life span developmental perspective (Leenaars, 1991c).

5. Among the factors in suicides among the older adults are depression, physical health problems and decline, an irrevocable loss of significant others (or ideals) through death and other circumstances, social isolation, hopelessness/helplessness and dependency, loss of social roles (e.g., employment), being a burden, sex roles, and a negative cultural attitude toward the elderly.

6. For the elderly to adjust (i.e., "attain successful aging") the individual needs to be flexible and adapt to the changing circumstances of his or her time-line (Richman, 1991). The older person, I believe, must be able to resolve the crisis of integrity versus despair in late adulthood (Erikson, 1963, 1968).

7. Suicide in the older adult, if it is understood, can be prevented (Leenaars, 1991c; Richman, 1991).

Suicide Notes: The Method

Early research (e.g., Wolff, 1931) on suicide notes largely utilized an anecdotal approach that incorporated descriptive information. Subsequent methods of study have primarily included classification analysis and content analysis. There are currently over 70 published articles on suicide notes. An extensive review with an annotated bibliography has been presented elsewhere (Leenaars, 1988a). Only a very few of these studies have utilized a theoretical–conceptual analysis, despite the assertion in the first formal study of suicide notes that such an approach offered much promise (Shneidman & Farberow, 1957). In a series of studies spanning the last 14 years (Leenaars, 1979, 1985, 1986, 1987, 1988a, 1988b, 1991a, 1991b; Leenaars & Balance, 1981, 1984b, 1984c; Leenaars, Balance, Wenckstern & Rudzinski, 1985), the author and his colleagues have applied a logical, empirical analysis to suicide notes. Our method permits a theoretical analysis of suicide notes and augments the effectiveness of previous controls.

Our method, which has been previously described in detail (Leenaars, 1988a; Leenaars & Balance, 1984b), treats the notes as an archival source. This source is subjected to the scrutiny of control hypotheses, following an ex post facto research design (Kerlinger, 1964). Suicide notes are recast in different theoretical contexts (hypotheses, theories, models, etc.), for which lines of evidence of each of these positions can then be pursued in the data, utilizing Carnap's logical and empirical procedures (1959) for such investigations. These positivistic procedures call for the translating of theoretical formulations into observable (specific) *protocol sentences* in order to test the formulations. The protocol sentences express the meaning of a given theory as they are matched empirically, by independent clinical judges, with the actual data. Next, conclusions are developed from the verified protocol sentences. To date, the theories of 10 suicidologists have been investigated (Leenaars, 1988a, 1989a, 1989b). Specifically, studies of A. Adler, L. Binswanger, S. Freud, C. G. Jung, K. A. Menninger, G. Kelly, H. A. Murray, E. S. Shneidman, H. S. Sullivan, and G. Zilboorg have been undertaken. The results of these studies regarding specific investigations of older adults will be presented next.

Suicide Notes of Older Adults: Nomothetic Findings

Our research (Leenaars, 1987, 1988a, 1989a, 1989b, 1991a) has indicated that, despite consistency in significant characteristics of suicide across the life span, older adults do differ from other adults in their suicide notes and, by implication, their suicides. Older adults differ from other adults in several essential characteristics. These differences are quantitative ones; the characteristics of suicide are largely the same across the entire life span. The following observations have been made:

Long-Term Instability. Old age by itself does not explain suicide. Indeed, *a* situational factor by itself does not explain suicide in the elderly. Although various situational factors (including age) can be identified in suicides, older (and young) adults who kill themselves exhibit long-term problems. Unlike most of the adult life span, older adults frequently describe in their suicide note a history to their death. These adults highlight in their notes that it is a myth that just age— or any situation—caused the death.

Older adults (and young adults) often see suicide as related to long-term instability. Evidence, for example, of alcoholism, multiple losses, and neuropsychiatric hospitalization is often evident in their notes. Their lives, like those of similar young adults, is seen as truncated because of their instability. They are unable to adapt to their history. I do not wish to suggest that there were direct one-to-one quotes of their inability to adjust in the notes, since these did not differ from most other adults'; rather, it was simply that they saw a long history to their unbearable pain, their despair.

Despite the similarity of long-term instability with young adults, the suicides of these older individuals are quite different from the suicides of young adults. Older adults' levels of perturbation and ambivalence about their deaths are much lower. They also exhibit less confusion about self (identity) than younger adults.

Older adults' levels of perturbation in their notes were low; they did not frequently report catastrophic levels of perturbation. They reported being able to handle pressures and feelings. For these older adults, unlike young adults, suicide was not seen as an inability to adjust to heightened emotions or pressures. They were not as frequently perturbed with the final solution. Suicide, I presume, was a relief.

Previous research, indeed, has indicated that older adults—much more so than other adults—*wish* to die when they choose death in the life–death decision (Farberow & Shneidman, 1957). My research shows that older adults are less ambivalent about suicide than young adults. There are fewer contradictory feelings, attitudes, and/or thrusts in their notes. If we read a suicide note, it appears that, to the author of the note, the situation is obvious: Life is painful and does not need to be borne. There may be long-term instability related to their wish for death, but just as they experience lower levels of perturbation, they are less ambivalent about death than young adults. Older adults' notes are very direct and obvious.

Again, despite the similarity in long-term instability, older adults also show less confusion about self (identity) than do young adults. They report being certain about themselves, experiencing less stress and less shame and loss of face. There appears to be less aggression directed inwards. Even their thinking is judged by clinicians to be less dichotomous (i.e., either/or) and less confusing. Thus, in summary,

although older adults' degree of long-term instability is equivalent to
young adults (and higher than most other adults), the characteristics
are qualitatively quite different in some important ways.
Indirect Expressions. Older suicidal adults wish to die. Their notes,
compared to individuals in young and middle adulthood, are less likely
to show evidence of redirected aggression, complications, and unconscious
implications. There are fewer contradictions and distortions and less
confusion. Their notes, in fact, are less frequently judged by clinicians
to contain confusion about perception of reality and nonreality. For
them, their notes are obvious. They report being aware more frequently
of the processes that led to their solution and, especially noteworthy,
there is a general trend toward clinicians seeing the suicide note (and
the suicide?) as less indirect. However, whether this translates, for
example, into unconscious processes being less of a factor is yet to be
studied. Such research is especially important, since a driving force in
most suicides are unconscious processes (Leenaars, 1986, 1988a, in progress; McLister & Leenaars, 1988).

These observations, I believe, are directly related to the older person's
wish to die. Farberow and Shneidman (1957), following Karl Menninger's
theory of suicide (1933, 1938), presented the psychodynamic motivations
underlying suicide: the wish to kill, the wish to be killed, and the wish
to die. Based on their results and the implications of the current findings,
it is the wish to die that is most relevant to the elderly. For Menninger
the "wish to die" was associated with hopelessness, fear, fatigue, and
despair. Menninger (1938) noted that the wish to die, conscious or
unconscious, is exceedingly widespread. Based on my own results, I
assume that the wish in the older adult is often conscious. These elderly
people, to quote from Menninger, "marshall almost unanswerable arguments for the desirability of dying" (p. 71). As I noted elsewhere
(1988), older suicidal adults argue directly, "with passionate eloquence
and with flawless logic (from their perspective) that life is hard, bitter,
futile and hopeless; that it entails more pain than pleasure; that there
is for them no profit or purpose in it and no conceivable justification
for living on" (p. 116). One patient of Menninger's (1938) stated this
as "Do not ask me why I should like to die. In a more energetic mood
I would defy you to tell me why I should live, but now I only wonder,
and even wonder is difficult when one has a preconceived conviction
in favor of death" (p. 76).

Farberow and Shneidman noted an important factor about this wish.
Older suicidal adults, in their letters, are less intense in affect and
their problems are more chronic. My results are consistent. Farberow
and Shneidman (1957) suggested that an elderly group exhibited "chronic
feelings of discouragement—pain . . . illness . . . *despair*" (italics added).

They wrote, "The older suicide is tired, bitter of life or of pain and suffering, and he writes that he is physically and/or mentally exhausted" (p. 47).

By way of reflection, the elderly person can be seen as trapped by despair. The notes of all age groups attest to unbearable pain, hopelessness, and helplessness. All this can be seen as the despair described by Erikson. However, integrity might still be possible with help or treatment. The state of despair is consistent with a presence of a treatable life situation: The pain can become bearable.

Relationships. The suicidal person is often seen as having problems in establishing and maintaining relationships. Suicidal people, in fact, frequently in their final letters describe a disturbed, unbearable interpersonal situation. Loss is important. A positive development in those same disturbed relations was held as the only possible way to go on living, but such a development was seen as not forthcoming. Suicide appears to be often related to unsatisfied or frustrated attachment needs (although other needs may also be evident; e.g., frustrations related to achievement, autonomy, dominance, perfection). Yet, surprisingly, such a process is different in some ways in older adults than other adults.

From a clinical perspective, we often see problems in attachments in our older suicidal patients. When I examined the pattern of relationships in suicide notes, a note-worthy observation emerged. Although generally there are no important psychological sex differences in suicide (Leenaars, 1987, 1988a, 1988b; Lester, 1989), when a sex by age perspective is taken on the dimension of relationships, the following was noted: Older females less frequently write about relationships than older males. The older males very often highlight the problems of relations. This pattern is the reverse in young and middle adulthood. In these time-lines it is the females who more frequently write about having problems in establishing and maintaining relationships. Thus the importance of relations in older adults appears to be more true for males although, alternatively, the loss may be less explicitly stated in the notes of females, raising the question, as previously noted, about the use of personal documents in science. Perhaps some of the important things behind a suicide is what is kept secret; maybe the suicidal act is the communication. Yet, as a strong proponent of personal documents, I would add as a footnote: We can only study what we have—the suicide note being the most personal revealing document in suicidology.

It would appear that, for older males, relationships were critical. They often describe a loss that is unbearable; for example, being a widower is seen as too much to bear. They saw the relation as helpful, sometimes essential. For example, for the widower, his wife's death makes death inviting. He cannot bear to live; in fact, in some notes one gets the impression that he does not know how. There is no reason to live. He wishes to die. It may well be that, in our Western culture many men are unable to adjust, to loss (e.g., of spouse, job, health). This observation is important because, as noted by McIntosh in this volume, it is especially elderly males who are at risk for death by suicide.

As an aside, the previous observation highlights for me that it is not only essential to adopt a developmental perspective, but that an age by sex developmental perspective may be helpful in understanding suicide in the elderly.

Observations about the need for attachment being a less frequent theme in the suicide notes of older women than those of older men is not to say that relationships are not important for the women. They are! Relationships are one of the most frequent themes in all suicidal notes. Richman, in this volume and elsewhere (e.g., Richman, 1991), has shown how critical family, friends, etc. are to elderly suicides, and I would add, to all people across the life span. In fact, I am of the tentative position that the need for attachment is the most critical unconscious process in suicide (Leenaars, in progress). It may well be the driving force behind many self-chosen deaths.

A Developmental View of Older Adults' Suicides

When one is attempting to understand the suicide of adults, developmental age (time-line) is a significant variable to be accounted for in that perspective or model. The suicide notes and, by implication, suicides of older adults are psychologically different from other adults despite, I suspect, even greater commonalities.

A life span developmental perspective is essential for understanding suicidal phenomena (Leenaars, 1991c), and no less so in the elderly. To recapitulate the findings within Erikson's framework, the following can be tentatively concluded:

Finitude of one's life is obvious to most older adults. In our older years we evaluate our life. We evaluate its meaning. For examples: Has one's life been marked by instability? Have I been intimate? Have I generated something? It would appear that the suicidal person, although not necessarily perturbed, despairs. They judge their life—their history—to have been too unstable. The damp, drizzly November in the soul is obvious to them. They are direct and not ambivalent: They wish to die.

Our suicidal older adults see no alternatives. Indeed, there are few alternatives or contradictions in their notes. They reject everything. All was a waste. One's relations (e.g., spouse, child, job) are often now meaningless. This latter observation is especially true for the males. Given their loss there is no integrity for them and they despair.

As a personal observation, after reading some 1,200 notes, I am struck by the lack of what Erikson calls wisdom in suicide notes. I am not suggesting this is surprising, only that developmentally there is a poverty of wit, knowledge, and mature judgment, something that is obvious in most other writings of our elderly people.

The notes are communications of despair. Although they wish to die, the suicidal older adult, by his plunge into death, does *not* accept death.

Erikson himself has not published much about suicide; the above are my speculations within his frame. However, in line with Erikson's position that death is "the most important overall aspect of life," he has recently made the following comment: "All old people simply have to accept approaching death as a daily problem. They see it happen to their relatives and friends and know that it is apt to suddenly come from somewhere when it was not expected. Their suicide, thus, is most of all *active* death: at least they have made the decision and the choice of time and place" (p. xii). This view is consistent with the wish to die. The suicide in late adulthood takes an active role in the demise. The older suicidal person sees suicide as a solution to pain and, according to Erikson (1989), this is an identity decision. Suicide is an identity. In this sense, the older suicidal person addresses previous dialectics. Suicide, Erikson (1989) states, "gives them an identity in life, even if it is an identity of one who brought about his own death" (p xii).

As a more general comment, the current formulation about older adults should not be construed to mean that development is simply discontinuous. Development across the life span is both *discontinuous* and *continuous* (Piaget, 1970). Adult development is dynamic, ongoing, and serial. The suicidal person does not respond anew to each crisis in his adult life, but one's reactions are consistent in many ways with that individual's previous reaction to loss, threat, impotence, etc. There is an *elliptical* nature to development (Shneidman, 1980, 1985). There is change and consistency. Our point here is simply that, within the adult life span, older adults' suicides are psychologically different from other adults, despite enormous commonalities across the life span.

Future research in the suicide notes of older adults is needed. Since suicide notes have been most rewarding in understanding suicide (Shneidman, 1985), more study is warranted. The current observations are only a beginning; in fact, that is all they are. Verification is needed.

As one avenue for study, I would suggest that a review of the research on suicide in the elderly be undertaken, *protocol sentences* be developed from this review, and a theoretical–conceptual analysis of suicide notes be undertaken.

Suicide Notes of Older Adults: Idiographic Summary

To summarize, a number of genuine suicide notes of older adults are presented. They allow us, from an idiographic point of view, to imagine what it was really like for these individuals as they engaged in the penultimate act.

1) My dear:
Please forgive me—but life is'nt worth living for me anymore.

I love you

Tell Susanne to forgive me too! And all my friends

2) Please dear god
Forgive me for taking my life. The real cause is my wife, who swindled me out of my money and my poor health which she caused.
If I die please call at the address mentioned below,
She resides as Mrs. _____ _____

_____ , _____ , _____
Last none phone number is, 000-0000,
Please call Dr. _____ _____ , _____ , Phone 000-0000.
Should I pass away please god forgive me. Will be pleased if the Windsor Park Memorial Chapel 1000 Windsor Ave. Phone no. 000-0000. If possible contact Temple Emmanual as we have our two daughters are laid away at the Temple Emmanual cementary would please me to be beside them.
I owe my sister _____ $300 to be paid. Her married name is Mrs.
_____ _____ Apt. _____
Phone 000-0000. Also notify Mr. and Mrs. _____ , _____
_____ , Phone 000-0000.
Please notify my dear cousins Mr. and Mrs. _____ _____
phone 000-0000 I am in hopes that the sale of my BMW automobile and the furniture will cover the expenses.
I always loved my wife and my children, but it impossible to please my wife.
Please allow my two sisters to take whatever food clothing furniture they are
Mrs. _____ _____ , _____ phone number 000-0000
Mrs. _____ _____ , _____ phone number 000-0000 God love you all
Your brother,
Bill

3) To whom it may concern—

If I take more sleeping pills than I should it is because I must—I will never get well and cannot accept my life as it is—My husband Bob has been an angel to me, doing more for me than anyone could believe—he is a wonderful man—

Please dispose of me as cheaply as possible—no fus—no tears—I need peace at last.

Mary

4) I had a stroke Feb; 1982. Aug. 1982 I heard of good news from the milkman. I have had arthritis, hardening of arteries ever since. Arthritis is getting worse. I just about can stand the pain. To whom it may concern. I want to thank you for the propaganda. I have a nice reputation. I want to thank you again for the kind words you said about me.

The next time you hear anything, keep your god damn mouth shut. I've been on this earth 5 years on borrowed time. I don't want to go to a Hospital or Home. I want keep the bills down, we haven't that kind of money 35.00 a day. I sooner be dead than alive.

Give me a cheap funeral. No flowers.

Bill

Dr. Doe—you have been good to me. I have been a poor patient

Lanny:

Put screws in cabinets before they come down and somebody gets hurt. There only hanging up there in the kitchen.

Bill

References

Allport, G. (1942). The *use of personal documents in psychological science*. New York: Social Science Research Council.

Butler, R. (1963). The life review: An interpretation of reminiscence in the aged. *Psychiatry, 26*, 65–76.

Carnap, R. (1959). Psychology in physical language. In A. Ayer (Ed.), *Logical positivism* (pp. 165–208). New York: Free Press. (Original published in 1931).

Colarusso, C., & Nemiroff, R. (1981). *Adult development*. New York: Plenum.

Darbonne, A. (1969). Suicide and age: A suicide note analysis. *Journal of Consulting and Clinical Psychology, 33*, 46–50.

Erikson, E. (1963). *Childhood and society* (2nd ed.). New York: Norton.

Erikson, E. (1964). *Insight and responsibility*. New York: Norton.

Erikson, E. (1968). *Identity: Youth and crisis*. New York: Norton.

Erikson, E. (1980). *Identity and the life cycle*. New York: Norton.

Erikson, E. (1989). Foreward. In D. Jacobs & H. Brown (Eds.), *Suicide: Understanding and responding* (pp. xi–xiv). Madison, CT: International Universities Press.

Farberow, N., & Shneidman, S. (1957). Suicide and age. In E. Shneidman & N. Farberow (Eds.), *Clues to suicide* (pp. 41–49). New York: McGraw-Hill.

Frager, R., & Fadiman, J. (1984). *Personality and personal growth* (2nd ed.). New York: Harper & Row.

Health and Welfare, Canada (1987). *Suicide in Canada*. Ottawa: Department of National Health and Welfare.

Kalish, R. (1975). *Late adulthood: Perspectives in human development*. Monterey, CA: Brooks/Cole.

Kerlinger, F. (1964). *Foundations of behavioral research*. New York: Holt, Rinehart & Winston.

Kimmel, D. (1974). *Adulthood and aging*. New York: Wiley.

Leenaars, A. (1979). *A study of the manifest content of suicide notes from three different theoretical perspectives: L. Binswanger, S. Freud, and G. Kelly*. Unpublished Ph.D. dissertation, Windsor, Canada.

Leenaars, A. (1985). Freud's and Shneidman's formulations of suicide investigated through suicide notes. In E. Shneidman (Chair), *Suicide notes and other personal documents in psychological science*. Symposium conducted at the meeting of the American Psychological Association, Los Angeles, CA.

Leenaars, A. (1986). A brief note on the latent content in suicide notes. *Psychological Reports, 59*, 640–642.

Leenaars, A. (1987). An empirical investigation of Shneidman's formulations regarding suicide: Age & sex. *Suicide & Life-Threatening Behavior, 17*, 233–250.

Leenaars, A. (1988a). *Suicide notes*. New York: Human Sciences Press.

Leenaars, A. (1988b). Are women's suicides really different from men's? *Women & Health, 18*, 17–33.

Leenaars, A. (1989a). Are young adults' suicides psychologically different from those of other adults? (The Shneidman lecture). *Suicide & Life-Threatening Behavior, 19*, 249–263.

Leenaars, A. (1989b). Suicide across the adult life-span: An archival study. *Crisis, 10*, 132–151.

Leenaars, A. (1991a). Suicide in the young adult. In A. Leenaars (Ed.), *Life span perspectives of suicide* (pp. 121–136). New York: Plenum.

Leenaars, A. (1991b). Suicide notes and their implications for intervention. *Crisis, 12*, 1–20.

Leenaars, A. (Ed.). (1991c). *Life span perspectives of suicide*. New York: Plenum.

Leenaars, A. (In progress). Orientations toward suicide: Unconscious processes. In A. Leenaars, P. Cantor, R. Litman, & R. Maris (Eds.), *Suicidology: Essays in honor of Edwin S. Shneidman*.

Leenaars, A., & Balance, W. (1981). A predictive approach to the study of manifest content in suicide notes. *Journal of Clinical Psychology, 37*, 50–52.

Leenaars, A., & Balance, W. (1984a). A predictive approach to suicide notes of young and old people from Freud's formulations regarding suicide. *Journal of Clinical Psychology, 40*, 1362–1364.

Leenaars, A., & Balance, W. (1984b). A logical empirical approach to the study of the manifest content in suicide notes. *Canadian Journal of Behavioral Science, 16*, 248–256.

Leenaars, A., & Balance, W. (1984c). A predictive approach to Freud's formulations regarding suicide. *Suicide & Life-Threatening Behavior, 14*, 275–283.

Leenaars, A., Balance, W., Wenckstern, S., & Rudzinski, D. (1985). An empirical investigation of Shneidman's formulations regarding suicide. *Suicide & Life-Threatening Behavior, 15*, 184–195.

Leenaars, A., & Lester, D. (1990). A comparison of rates and patterns of suicide for Canada and the United States, 1960–1985. In D. Lester (Ed.), *Suicide '90* (pp. 21–22). Denver, CO: American Association of Suicidology.

Lester, D. (1989). Sex differences in the motives expressed in suicide notes. *Perceptual and Motor Skills, 69*, 642.

Lester, D. (1991). Suicide across the life span: A look at international trends. In A. Leenaars (Ed.), *Life span perspectives of suicide* (pp. 71–80). New York: Plenum.

Lester, D., & Hummel, H. (1980). Motives for suicide in elderly people. *Psychological Reports, 47*, 870.

Lester, D., & Reeve, C. (1982). The suicide notes of young and old people. *Psychological Reports, 50*, 334.

Maddox, G. (1987). *The encyclopedia of aging.* New York: Springer.

Maris, R. (1981). *Pathways to suicide.* Baltimore, MD: The Johns Hopkins University Press.

Menninger, K. (1933). Psychoanalytic aspects of suicide. *The International Journal of Psycho-analysis, 14*, 376–390.

Menninger, K. (1938). *Man against himself.* New York: Harcourt, Brace & Co.

McIntosh, J. (1991). Epidemiology of suicide in the United States. In A. Leenaars (Ed.), *Life span perspectives of suicide* (pp. 55–69). New York: Plenum.

McLister, B., & Leenaars, A. (1988). An empirical investigation of the latent content in suicide notes. *Psychological Reports, 63*, 238.

Neugarten, B., Moore, J., & Lowe, J. (1965). Age norms, age constraints, and adult socialization. *American Journal of Sociology, 70*, 710–717.

Osgood, N., & McIntosh, J. (1986). *Suicide and the elderly: An annotated bibliography and review.* Westport CT: Greenwood Press.

Peck, R. (1956). Psychological developments in the second half of life. In J. Anderson (Ed.), *Psychological aspects of aging.* Washington, DC: American Psychological Association.

Piaget, J. (1970). *Structuralism* (C. Maschler, Trans.). New York: Harper & Row.

Richman, J. (1991). Suicide and the elderly. In A. Leenaars (Ed.), *Life span perspectives of suicide* (pp. 153–167). New York: Plenum.

Runyan, W. (1982). In defense of the case study method. *American Journal of Orthopsychiatry, 53*, 440–446.

Shneidman, E. (1980). *Voices of death.* New York: Harper & Row.

Shneidman, E. (1985). *Definition of suicide.* New York: Wiley.

Shneidman, E., & Farberow, N. (1957). *Clues to suicide.* New York: McGraw-Hill.

Tuckman, J., Kleiner, R., & Lavell, M. (1959). Emotional content of suicide notes. *American Journal of Psychiatry, 116*, 59–63.

U.S. Dept. of Health and Human Services, National Center for Health Statistics (1990). Mortality detail files, 1979–1980 (Vol. II), 1982–1982 (Vol. III), 1983–1984 (Vol. IV), 1985 (Vol. V), and 1986–1987 (Vol. VI) (computer file). Ann Arbor, MI: Inter-university Consortium for Political and Social Research (producer and distributor).

Windelband, W. (1904). *Geschichte und haturwissenschaft.* Strassburg, Germany: Heitz.

Wolff, H. (1931). Suicide notes. *American Mercury, 24*, 264–272.

6

Gender and Suicide in the Elderly

Silvia Sara Canetto, PhD
Colorado State University

ABSTRACT: Gender is one of the most important predictors of suicide in the elderly. In North America, older women are less likely to be suicidal than older men. So far, suicidologists have either ignored gender differences or have focused on the presumed causes of older men's suicidal behavior. In this paper, the focus is on older women's low rates of suicidal mortality. On the basis of a review of the literature, several hypotheses are suggested. One is that gender differences in suicide mortality reflect differences in coping. Another hypothesis is that gender differences are influenced by gender norms of suicidal behavior. Directions for prevention are proposed.

Despite decades of scholarship on suicidal behavior in the elderly (see reviews by Kirsling, 1986; Lyons, 1984), and an even larger body of literature on gender and suicidal behavior (see reviews by Lester, 1969; Lester, 1979; Linehan, 1971; Neuringer, 1982; Wilson, 1981), very little work (Breed & Huffine, 1979) has been done to examine the interrelationship between the two. Theories of elderly suicide typically have been formulated in terms of a gender-neutral elderly person (Miller, 1978) or in terms of elderly males (Cath, 1980). Yet gender is one of the most important predictors of suicide in the elderly. In North America, older women are less likely to die of suicide than older men (McIntosh, this issue).

An earlier version of this article was presented at the pre-conference seminar, *Suicide and the Elderly*, held at the convention of the American Association of Suicidology, Boston, MA, in April, 1991. My thanks go to the editors of this special issue for helpful feedback on this revision, and to colleagues and friends Valerie Assetto, Julie Beyers, Karen Fondacaro, Jeremy Gersovitz, David Lester, Laura Solomon, and David Wohl for reading and commenting on different versions of this article.

Correspondence concerning this article should be addressed to Silvia Sara Canetto, Department of Psychology, Colorado State University, Fort Collins, CO 80523.

In this paper, the dimensions of gender and aging are central to an analysis of the theoretical and empirical literature on suicidal behavior. In contrast to the previous literature on elderly suicide, women's resilience rather than men's vulnerability will be the primary question. Attention to the characteristics of survivors rather than the liabilities of casualties may help with planning effective intervention and prevention. In recognition of the variations in rates and meanings of suicide in different countries, this paper will focus on research and theories from the North American (U.S. and Canadian) and British literature.

With regard to nomenclature, suicidal acts that resulted in the person's death will be referred to as "fatal" or "lethal" suicide acts—rather than "completed" or "successful" suicides, as they are often called in the North American literature. Suicidal acts that did not result in the person's death will be referred to as "nonlethal" or "nonfatal" suicidal acts—in lieu of the terms "attempted suicide" and "parasuicide" commonly used in the North American and British literature, respectively. As pointed out by Chesler (1972) and Lester (1989), a disadvantage of the traditional nomenclature is that it defines as successful a suicidal act in which the person dies; conversely, it erroneously implies that all persons who engage in life-threatening behavior attempt or intend to die. The term suicidal behavior, not otherwise specified, will be used in a traditional manner, that is, as an inclusive term refering to both fatal and nonfatal suicidal behavior, or whenever information is not available on whether one is dealing with fatal or nonfatal suicidal behavior.

Epidemiology

Complete information about gender patterns of death by suicidal behavior in the elderly is not readily available. The two main sources, national official suicide statistics and local epidemiological studies, have serious limitations. Neither source systematically categorizes all the information by both gender and age. On the one hand, official suicide statistics do not include information on variables such as occupation, socioeconomic status, or living circumstances (McIntosh, 1989). On the other hand, local epidemiological surveys typically include a broad range of variables but may be less representative of national figures. Furthermore, according to Kushner (1985), fatal suicidal behavior may be underreported for women due to a bias against recording women's death as suicide.

The available evidence (see McIntosh, this issue, for a thorough review) indicates that, in North America, older women are less likely than older men to die as a result of suicidal acts. For white women, rates of lethal suicide tend to peak around age 50 (Diggory, 1976; Manton, Blazer, & Woodbury, 1987). For non-white women, rates of lethal suicide remain low and fairly constant throughout adulthood and old age (Manton et al., 1987). Men age 60 and over have the highest suicide mortality of any age group (Manton et al., 1987), even though rates for young adults have recently been increasing faster than the rates for other age groups. Until recently, white males had the highest rate of lethal suicides; for white males, the peak risk periods are ages 45 to 50 and around age 80 (Manton et al., 1987). New studies, however, suggest that non-white males may be at great risk as well (Manton et al., 1987). Social isolation (Miller, 1978), living alone, being unmarried (single, separated, divorced or widowed—see Stenback, 1980, for a review), unemployed, and/or retired (Gardner, Bahn, & Mack, 1964; Stenback, 1980) are considered risk factors for suicidal death in older men.

Patterns of nonfatal suicidal behavior in late life are much more difficult to determine due to the lack of systematic and reliable archival data. It is usually reported that nonfatal suicidal behavior diminishes with age (e.g., Wilson, 1981). There is also evidence suggesting that, after age 65, men may equal (Pierce, 1987) and even outnumber women in rates of nonfatal suicidal acts (Jarvis, Ferrence, Johnson, & Whitehead, 1976).

Why are Older Women Less Suicidal than Older Men?

Physical Factors

Physical Strength

Earlier theories suggested that women are less likely to die of suicide because they are physically weaker than men (Lester, 1969): "The acts of firing a gun, plunging a knife, or kicking a chair away may be all the more difficult for a woman because of her lesser strength" (p. 342).

The possibility that the gender differences in suicidal mortality are due to difference in physical strength has been discredited (Lester, 1979). No particular physical fitness is required to pull a trigger. In fact men are most dangerous to themselves after age 75, when they are most physically frail.

Sex Hormones

Much attention has been devoted to the role of sex hormones in the suicidal behavior of women, and very little to the role of sex hormones in the suicidal behavior of men.

One of the most popular theories is that women's suicidal behavior is related to the menstrual cycle. Research on the association between menstrual stages and suicidal behavior has persisted despite the lack of consistent evidence (see Neuringer & Lettieri, 1982, and Lester, 1988, for reviews). Changes in levels of estrogen and progesterone, premenstrual cramps, "menstrual messiness," and the presumed "help-lessness" of menstruation have all been considered plausible precipitants of suicidal behavior. Similarly, the physiology of pregnancy has been investigated for links to suicide. The most peculiar aspect of these theories is the assumption of a connection between women's *normal* reproductive system physiology and psychopathology—an assumption that is reminiscent of the Victorian medical theory that women are vulnerable to periodic "reflex insanity" (Showalter, 1985). Interestingly, menopause has not attracted the attention of biological suicidologists. One reason may be that in the United States, suicidal behavior declines past midlife for women, a fact that challenges the assumption of intrinsic biopsychological weakness in women.

In contrast to the literature on suicide and female physiology, sex hormones have not been promoted as an explanation of suicidal behavior in men. The connection between reproductive physiology and "nervous disorders" is rarely made from men. Yet, one could easily postulate that older males' high rates of suicidal death are the result of a chronic *deficit* in estrogen or the toxic influence of testosterone.

Physical Illness

Physical illness or disability are often cited among the factors as-sociated with suicide in the elderly (e.g., Sainsbury, 1963). According to the review of studies by Stenback (1980), physical illness plays less of a role in nonfatal than in fatal suicides.

A majority of older individuals who become sick and/or disabled do not kill themselves; therefore, the question is: What sets apart those individuals who become suicidal? According to a review of studies by Lyons (1984), characteristics that may interact with the illness and thus increase the risk of suicide include a strong need to be active and independent, a history of depression and hostility, and a proclivity toward brooding. The literature does not address whether physical illness is more of a precipitant of suicide for older men than for older women.

Psychological Factors

Psychological Complexity and Flexibility

Several suicidologists have attributed women's lower rates of suicidal deaths to their being psychologically simple, mentally dull, passive, conforming, and suggestible. It has been said that women are not im-aginative and intellectually complex enough to kill themselves (Durkheim, 1951); that they unquestionably accept traditional and religious prohibitions against suicide (Davis, 1904; Durkheim, 1897/1951); and that they passively accept the blows of life more readily than men (Durkheim, 1951; Neuringer & Lettieri, 1982). Men, on the other hand, being imaginative, critical, and in control, affirm themselves against adversity by killing themselves. These explanations have been extended to geriatric suicides. Passivity, suggestibility, and malleability were proposed by Breed and Huffine (1979) as the personality characteristics underlying older women's low rates of suicidal death.

It is interesting to note that the characteristics women display are pejoratively labeled, even if they are associated with adaptation and survival, and whatever characteristics men display are positively labeled, even when they lead to self-destruction. It is also worth noting that the same characteristics that are lauded in suicidal men may be described as pathogenic when studied independent of gender. In this regard, research on thinking in suicidal persons has suggested that suicidal individuals are less—not more—imaginative, less differentiated, and less mentally flexible than nonsuicidal individuals (see Levenson, 1974, for a review). According to research by Neuringer, Levenson, and Kaplan (1971), the suicidal person's rigid and polarized style of thinking is a lifelong dispositional tendency rather than a transient reaction to stress.

An alternative hypothesis is that women may be capable of more complex and flexible coping than men. According to Breed and Huffine (1979), women's flexibility is the result of socialization and developmental experiences. Many women experience several role shifts during adulthood: "As the child progresses through the developmental stages . . . the demands of the mother's role qualitatively shift and change. In addition, during this period of mothering, the woman may well be in and out of the labor market, further varying her roles" (p. 302). On the other hand, for many men, adult development tends to follow a relatively stable course, with work remaining a constant and often exclusive focus. According to Breed and Huffine (1979), a man "is not likely to experience major qualitative change after the first few years of adulthood and marriage. In his developmental process, each stage prepares him for the next, and the demands and expectations on him are consistent throughout—he is expected to be assertive, to seek mastery over his environment, and to strive for achievement" (p. 302).

Clinging to Life

Another theory of gender differences in rates of suicidal death is that women cling to life more than men (Schneider, 1954, cited in Lester, 1969). If one takes life expectancy as a measure of clinging to life, one may indeed conclude that women hold on to life more than men: Women have a seven-year advantage in life expectancy over men (Smith, 1990). Women are less likely than men to engage in self-destructive life-styles, such as chronic use of alcohol and illicit drugs (Canetto, in press) or criminality (Al-Issa, 1982), or to die a violent death, such as in a motor vehicle accident or a homicide (Holinger, 1987). Whether women's avoidance of violent life-styles and deaths should be viewed as biological (Schneider, 1954, cited in Lester, 1969) or psychological clinging to life, socialized behavior or healthy resilience is debatable.

Intent

Gender differences in suicidal mortality are sometimes attributed to differences in intent. It has been postulated that women are more "manipulative" than men, and that they use suicide to communicate hostility or helplessness, not to achieve death, as do men (Stengel, 1964). According to Stengel, this is determined in part by the fact that other means of influence, such as physical intimidation, are not at their disposal to the same degree as to men. In any case, it is very plausible that many suicidal women do not intend to die; if more did, more would probably die. However, it is also very plausible that many men who died of suicide really intended to call for help, but their suicide "failed" and they actually killed themselves.

Not much is known about gender differences in suicidal intent in the elderly. There is some evidence suggesting that at least with regard to fatal suicides, older women and men may be similar in terms of expressed intent. In a classic study of suicide notes, Farberow and Shneidman (1957) found that a majority of older female and male suicidal victims had communicated an intent to die.

Psychological Disorders

Suicidal behavior is sometimes considered a manifestation of a psychological disorder. According to a review of studies by Stenback (1980), the percentages of suicidal individuals diagnosed as mentally disordered varies from 20% to 100%, depending on the stringency of the criteria.

The psychological condition most typically associated with suicidal behavior is depression (Stenback, 1980). Depression is more common in women than in men in adulthood (Weissman & Klerman, 1977), but not in late life, when rates of depression are the same for both women and men. Many investigators have suggested that this leveling of gender differences reflects declining rates for older women rather than increasing rates for older men (see George, 1990, for a review). Another condition often associated with suicide is alcoholism. According to Stenback (1980), chronic alcohol abuse is more commonly seen in nonlethal suicides than in lethal suicides, particularly among males over 65. However, chronic alcoholism is more commonly associated with nonfatal suicides under age 65 than with nonfatal suicides over age 65.

In sum, depression and alcoholism have been associated with suicidal behavior in the elderly. Most studies of the suicidal elderly do not provide information on diagnosis by gender; there is, however, some evidence suggesting that both depression and alcohol abuse are common among older suicidal males.

Help-Seeking

According to another perspective, women are less likely to die of suicide because they are more likely to seek professional help. Studies of utilization of suicide prevention facilities have confirmed an association of availability of suicide prevention centers with reduction of suicide risk in women, especially young adult white women (Miller, Coombs, Leeper, & Barton, 1984).

Mental health services are underused by the elderly, and according to a study by Conwell, Rotenberg, & Caine (1990), by elderly male suicides in particular. Some researchers, however (Barraclough, 1971; Miller, 1978), have observed that geriatric suicides are likely to occur after a recent visit to a physician. In an English study by Barraclough (1971), half of the individuals over 65 had seen their physician within a week of death, and 90% had done so during the preceding 3 months. In Miller's research (1978), as many as 75% of the older men studied had visited their physician within a month of their suicidal acts. These data suggest that it is not simply that suicidal women are more willing to seek professional help, but rather that they are more likely to seek the appropriate kind of help for psychological problems. Older men may be less comfortable acknowledging psychological difficulties, and thus may tend to express such problems through physical symptoms. If their physician is not trained to recognize a suicidal crisis under the physical complaints, or does not act on it, the client's denial may be reinforced and the risk for lethal outcome may be enhanced.

Social and Economic Factors

Social Status

Suicide among elderly men appears to be more common among lower-than among middle- and upper-class males (Bock & Webber, 1972; Gardner et al., 1964; Sainsbury, 1963), but the relationship between suicide and social status is far from established. There is evidence (Gardner et al., 1964) suggesting that some middle-class men slip into the lower class before the suicide. It has been suggested that upper- and middle-class individuals are advantaged by their greater economic, work, and retirement options (Breed & Huffine, 1979). The same authors also cite evidence suggesting that adaptation to old age may be more difficult in working-class individuals, if they had been raised in an environment stressing conformity and dependence on external authority.

Theories of social status have yet to be applied to older women's suicidal behavior.

Poverty

Suicidal behavior in the elderly has been attributed to poverty (Stenback, 1980). Poverty is related to social class, because social class is constructed primarily on the basis of occupation and income.

In the United States, older women are more likely to experience financial strain than older men (Hess, 1990). Women age 65 and over who live alone have a median income of $8,000, slightly higher if they are white, and only $5,000 if they are African-American. This is in contrast to a median income of $21,000 for white married couples. Households headed by older women are almost twice as likely as those headed by older men to have incomes below the poverty level of $5,500 for a single person over age 65, $6,900 for a two-person household. According to Hess (1990), these figures underestimate true poverty among older women, because many poor women move in with a child or become homeless.

Therefore, once gender is taken into account, the relation between poverty and suicide is no longer unequivocal. Older women are more likely to be poor but less likely to be suicidal than older men. One possible difference may be that, for many women, limited access to financial resources has been a longstanding problem, while for many men financial worries are unknown until retirement. Thus, for older men, having financial difficulties often is a new experience, while for women it may be something to which they have already "adapted." This suggests that a drop in income after achieving financial security may be more demoralizing and perhaps suicidogenic than chronic financial precariousness. Another possibility is that financial difficulties may be more humiliating for men than for women due to the emphasis on the male provider role.

Retirement

Suicidal behavior has been associated with retirement. According to this theory, retirement is suicidogenic because it brings about changes in income, social status, and family roles (Kirsling, 1986; Lyons, 1984).

The literature on retirement and suicide has described retirement from a male's point of view. It is usually argued that (for men) retirement implies a loss in income, prestige, meaningful and structured activity, and interpersonal relationship (Lyons, 1984; Miller, 1978). Role ambiguity may be created. As Lyons puts it: "there are no longer superiors to admire one's work and offer promotions and no positions . . . to seek" (p. 381).

Women, like men, go through retirement at midlife. Retirement may mean different things depending upon whether the woman is employed or not. For employed women, the issues of retirement are probably similar to those faced by employed men. For women, especially for homemakers, retirement may mean retirement from the reproductive and parental roles. Menopause and the children's departure from home would be its markers. A particularly severe loss of meaningful roles may be created for women whose self-esteem centered around being a mother (Suter, 1976). Retirement for many older women may also mean adapting to the husband's retirement and adjusting to his presence in the home territory. Coping with the husband's difficulties with retirement may exacerbate the wife's stress. A peak in suicide rates for women and men at midlife suggests that the years around retirement (ages 45 to 55 for women and ages 65 and over for men) may be quite demanding for both.

In sum, retirement is associated with changes in social status and family roles. For many men, especially men from older cohorts, these changes may be precipitated by retirement from employment; for women, these changes may be triggered by lessened involvement with parenting, and in younger cohorts, retirement from employment or both. These changes may explain the increased vulnerability to suicide for both women and men at midlife. For women this vulnerability to suicide appears to be over by age 55, while for men it seems to continue into older ages.

Living Alone

Living alone is frequently assumed to be a precipitant of suicidal behavior among the elderly (Sainsbury, 1962). This theory is thought to apply equally to older women and men. No empirical studies to date have examined this issue in terms of gender directly. However, a review of information on elderly persons' living arrangements by gender suggests that living alone may be a better predictor of suicidal behavior for older men than for older women.

Older women are much more likely to live alone than older men (see Hess, 1990, for a review). There are 6.5 million women age 65 and over living alone, in contrast to fewer than 2 million men. In the United States, women age 65 and over are almost half as likely as their male age-peers to be married. Women living alone are at higher risk of being placed in an institution than men, especially if they become physically unable to care for their household. Only 18% of disabled wives are cared for by their spouses, in contrast to 55% of disabled husbands.

In sum, older women are more likely to live alone, but they are less likely to be suicidal than older men. One reason may be that living alone may be more normative for older women than older men. Another reason may be that older men who live alone tend to be more isolated than older women who live alone (Stenback, 1980).

Bereavement and Widowhood

Many have linked suicide to the loss of a spouse (Kirsling, 1986; Lyons, 1984). Risk for suicide is considered to be particularly high in the first 6 weeks after the loss and when bereavement is associated with alcoholism (Essa & Howell-Burke, 1984). Risk may remain elevated for up to 5 years following bereavement (see Lyons, 1984, for a review).

Although widowhood is a predictor of suicide in both women and men, the effect seems to be stronger for men than for women. In the United States, females age 65 and over are 3.5 times more likely to be widowed than their male age peers. Older widows are also less likely to have the opportunity to remarry than older widowers. Widowers, however, are at higher suicidal risk than are widows (Bock & Webber, 1972; MacMahon & Pugh, 1965).

One reason bereavement is associated with greater risk of suicide for males than for females may be that many older men depend on their wives for emotional support. Older women appear to have more emotional connections with friends than do older men (Zarit, 1980). Although men have a greater quantity of social contacts through work, it appears that these contacts lack the quality of emotional support that women's contacts have. Losing a spouse may thus disrupt social support and emotional functioning more for a man than for a woman.

Another reason may be that many older men depend on their wives for their personal care and the running of a home. For many men, losing a spouse may involve becoming responsible for their personal and household care for the first time. Losing a spouse may thus disrupt personal stability and physical well-being more for a man than for a woman.

It is important to remember that for women, too, losing a spouse involves stress and discontinuities. For example, many women depend on their husbands for financial security and the management of the family assets. Becoming a widow may involve being responsible for one's own finances for the first time. Losing a spouse rarely threatens a man's financial status the way it does for a woman.

Overall, the data on geriatric elderly suicide are consistent with data on suicide and marital status through adulthood: Marriage is better protection against suicide for men than for women (Gove, 1972).

Sociocultural Factors

Method

A common assumption in the past has been that women's greater rates of suicide survival are due to their use of less lethal methods.

Method was traditionally seen as an indicator of intent. It was believed that women are less intent on killing themselves and thus choose methods that leave more room for rescue (Dublin, 1963; Furst & Ostow, 1979).

A challenge to this view has come from the work of Marks and Abernathy (1974) and Marks and Stokes (1976). Their respective studies of suicide methods by gender and region suggest that socialization and familiarity with various methods is a more powerful determinant of method choice than gender alone. In the American South, for example, Marks and Abernathy found that firearms are the most common method of suicide for both women and men.

Choice of method also varies according to cross-cultural and historical circumstances. In Asian-Americans, for example, suicide by hanging is being replaced by suicide by firearms, concomitant with the individual's degree of assimilation into the American culture (McIntosh & Santos, 1986). Similarly, in England and Wales there has been a decrease in female suicide by overdose and an increase in suicide by vehicle-exhaust poisoning and suffocation (McClure, 1987).

Only one study of methods of elderly suicide by gender is available (McIntosh & Santos, 1986). Overall, McIntosh and Santos' findings confirm prior evidence that the association between method and intent may be mediated by cultural accessibility. For example, in the United States, older white females are more likely to use poison, older black females firearms, and older non-white (but not black) females hanging; McIntosh and Santos also noted an increase in use of firearms in most of the groups studied, an indication perhaps of diminishing cultural distinctiveness and easier access to firearms.

Gender-Appropriate Deviance

According to sociocultural perspectives, the frequency of and mortality from suicidal behavior in women and men at different stages of life are influenced by social rules about gender- and age-appropriate deviance.

It has been suggested that, in many Western cultures, nonlethal suicides are more common in women because such acts are considered "feminine;" while lethal suicides are more common in men because they are considered "masculine" (Dublin, 1963; Linehan, 1973; Neuringer & Lettieri, 1982; Wilson, 1981). According to Suter (1976), nonlethal suicide is "feminine," since it combines personal helplessness with the idea of rescue by someone else. Says Chesler (1972): "Suicide attempts are the grand rites of 'femininity', i.e., ideally, women are supposed to 'lose' in order to 'win.' Women who succeed at suicide are, tragically, outwitting or rejecting their 'feminine' role, and at the only price possible: their death" (p. 49). Neuringer and Lettieri (1982) state that "suicidal gestures are an expected, and even socially sanctioned, behavior in unhappy women" and that "their attempts certainly receive less disapproval than similar behavior in men" (p. 22). They argue that it is more acceptable for women to express their emotions and needs and ask for help; while for men, the expectations are "to be strong, stolid and not to publicly express their weaknesses" (p. 22).

The "femininity" of nonlethal suicides and the "masculinity" of lethal suicides have been supported by studies by Linehan (1973) and White and Stillion (1988). On the basis of her observations, Linehan (1973) speculated that social acceptability influences the kind of suicide chosen when suicidal behavior is considered an option. For women, the social acceptance of nonlethal suicidal acts may promote chronic self-injurious behaviors, while social pressure against suicidal death may be a deterrent to killing oneself. Conversely, for men, the pressure against surviving suicide may lead them to act out the most drastic and dangerous of suicidal acts, even if their crisis is relatively minor and their intention is not to die. White and Stillion (1988) studied the reactions to troubled suicidal and nonsuicidal targets and found males to be most unsympathetic to suicidal male targets, while females were equally sympathetic to all troubled targets. According to White and Stillion, "attempted suicide by troubled males may be viewed by other males as violations of the sex-role message of strength, decisiveness, success, and inexpressiveness" (p. 365).

It is also possible that suicide is more common among the elderly than among the young, because historically suicide has been considered a reasonable solution for older individuals (Osgood, 1985). With regard to attitudes toward nonfatal suicide, there is evidence suggesting that nonfatal suicides are thought to be most "understandable" when performed by older women (Stillion, White, Edwards, & McDowell, 1989). The same study also found that older women received the least amount of sympathy and young women the most sympathy for their nonfatal suicidal behavior.

In sum, studies on the acceptability of suicide suggest that elderly males may be encouraged to kill themselves by cultural norms defining lethal suicide as masculine and developmentally reasonable. For elderly females, the social norms regarding suicidal behavior appear to be complex and contradictory.

Discussion

Older women are less likely to kill themselves than older men. Do older women have special advantages that protect them from suicide? An adequate answer to this question is not possible at this time given the scarcity of pertinent empirical data. On the basis of this literature review, it is, however, possible to suggest some preliminary hypotheses.

First, social and economic factors are not likely to account for older women's resilience. In fact, many older women live in conditions that, in older men, have been thought to precipitate suicidal behavior. For example, older women tend to live alone following divorce and widowhood; they also tend to have fewer financial resources than men.

Retirement and physical health factors do not explain women's resilience either. For many women, as for men, the transition to retirement is difficult. Older women, like older men, experience physical illnesses and disabilities. According to a review by Hess (1990), older men are more likely than older women to be able to afford costly medical services, to have short hospitalizations, and to have a spouse who can care for them at home. Older women tend to remain longer in acute-care beds and to be transferred to long-term care facilities or discharged to the care of an adult daughter or other female relatives. Older women are also more likely than men to end up in nursing homes: Three out of four nursing home residents are women.

What then accounts for older women's relatively low rates of suicidal deaths? There are indications that gender differences in coping may be important with regard to risk for suicidal behavior. Specifically, older women may have a more flexible and diverse ways of coping than older men: Compared to older men, older women may be more willing and capable of adopting different coping strategies—"passive" or "active," "connected" or "independent"—depending on the situation. There is evidence to suggest that women's flexible coping is not innate, but rather the product of socialization and developmental experiences.

One component of flexible coping involves the capacity and/or willingness to accommodate and adapt to situations. As Breed and Huffine (1979) have suggested, older women may be more capable and willing to adopt "passive" coping strategies than older men. Gender differences in adaptability and willingness to compromise are likely to be the result of socialization and developmental experiences (see Suter, 1976, for a review). Women are socialized to be sensitive to and to make room for other people's needs. Partly as a result of this, women's development involves many role changes and conflicts. Women are also discouraged from using aggression for conflict resolution. Finally, unlike men, many women experience significant changes in body functioning during adulthood—for example, when they become mothers—an experience that may prepare them for physical changes in late life (Breed & Huffine, 1979). Men, on the other hand, are socialized to always try to be in control and "shape the world" according to their needs. Whenever a conflict with others arises, men are likely to be encouraged to use forceful means to assert their will. As a result, men may come to late life with unrealistic expectations and a limited range of coping strategies. Being accustomed to controlling work and money, they may find the economic and work restrictions associated with retirement threatening. Having experienced their bodies functioning as fairly constant through adulthood, men may find the experience of physical aging disturbing.

Another component of flexible coping involves the capacity and/or willingness to be active, resourceful, and independent. Many older women may have had a limited experience with being financially independent and often suffer economic hardship following divorce and widowhood (Holt & Datan, 1984). However, most older women have extensive experience being active, resourceful, and independent with regard to personal care and socioemotional needs (see Troll & Turner, 1979, for a review). Most older women are also used to taking care of their households. After being responsible for the emotional and social welfare of their families, many older women maintain a well-developed network of friends. On the other hand, many men have extensive experience taking care of themselves financially but limited experience being active and resourceful with regard to taking care of their personal needs (Troll & Turner, 1979). Most men depend on women for their personal care and emotional well-being. Many men also rely on women for their social needs, such as keeping in touch with friends and family. Many men defer to women regarding the responsibility for their most personal relationships, most notably the emotional and practical responsibilities of being a parent. As a result, men may come to late life with a limited range of interpersonal skills and a total dependence on women for emotional connectedness. Having been nurtured all their lives by women, many men may not even have developed an appreciation for their own emotional needs. Having been socialized to expect being taken care of by women, they may experience taking care of themselves as abandonment. Without their partners, they may be unable or unwilling to provide themselves with even the most basic physical care, psychological sustenance, and social contacts.

So far it has been argued that socialization influences risk for suicide through its effects on coping. Socialization may also have an impact on suicide through definitions of gender-appropriate suicides. There is evidence that suicidal death in older men may be reinforced by an association of lethal suicide with masculinity and aging (Linehan, 1973; Stillion et al., 1989; White & Stillion, 1988). Older men may correctly anticipate being ridiculed and disliked if they survive suicide. On the other hand, suicidal behavior may be discouraged in older women by contradictory norms and the expectation of low sympathy.

Gender differences in coping and suicide rates have implications for the prevention of suicide. In terms of primary prevention, the focus should be on gender socialization experiences and roles. Traditionally, work has been considered the key to men's mental health. Thus, the typical recommendation for suicide prevention has been to keep men busy. For example, Osgood (1985) has suggested that men be given the opportunity to extend their working years past age 65. In principle, it maybe a good idea not to force men or women to retire on the basis of chronological age. Some individuals are interested and able to work past age 65. At the same time, for men to continue investing all of their energies into work as a way to "avoid" suicide may be a regressive solution.

It is very likely that relationships, not work, are the key to suicide prevention in older men. Social isolation and living alone (Stenback, 1980) are considered risk factors for suicidal death in older men. It may be that older men are most prone to suicide when relationships, not work, are missing (Cumming & Lazar, 1981). Thus, what older men may benefit from is relationship experiences and responsibilities. Relationship experiences may promote the flexibility of coping and socioemotional connectedness that many women enjoy. Furthermore, feeling responsible for a relationship may be a greater incentive to live than feeling responsible for a job. It has been argued that women are less likely to kill themselves because they consider the effect of their suicides on their loved ones (Kaplan & Klein, 1989). A man who feels responsible for another person's well-being might reject suicide just because that person could be upset by it.

An emphasis on relationships does not imply that work is not important to a person's mental health. Rather, a balance of work and relationship commitments may be the best protection against suicidal despair. This balance may be most easily achieved if both women and men are encouraged to pursue a variety of interests and talents, within and across gender roles. Meaningful participation in the world of labor has diminished women's vulnerability to emotional disorders (see Kaplan & Klein, 1989, for a review). It is very well likely that assuming relationship responsibilities will strengthen men's emotional resilience, including the resilience to suicide.

In terms of secondary prevention, two factors seem crucial: the ability to ask for help and the response to the call for help. While it is most important to ensure that suicidal men become more capable of seeking appropriate help, it will also be important to make sure that professionals become more sensitive to indirect clues of suicidal intent. A key person in this role is the physician. Research (Barraclough, 1971; Miller, 1978) has indicated that as many as 75% of suicidal elder persons visit their physicians before killing themselves. Education of the physician in the recognition and psychological management of the suicidal client will be necessary. Physicians should be aware that depression and suicidal behavior in the elderly may be masked by vague physical complaints (Essa & Howell-Burke, 1984; Victoroff, 1984). Physicians should also be careful about prescribing potentially lethal drugs, as a majority of those attempting suicide by overdose obtained the drugs from their physicians (Benson & Brodie, 1975).

Several directions for research by be fruitful. To learn more about women's successful coping, it might be useful to study older women who, according to traditional male parameters, should be at risk of suicide but are not, and unravel the source of their resilience. To learn more about the development of men's suicide vulnerability, it might be interesting to explore the relation between gender-role adherence and late-life suicidal behavior. One would expect older men who kill themselves to be fairly conventional with regard to gender-role expectations. It might also be interesting to explore gender-role rigidity in the families of origin and personal background of men who die of suicide. One would expect suicidal men to come from a cultural background in which adherence to sex-roles was highly valued.

References

Al-Issa, I. (1982). Gender and psychopathology in perspective. In I. Al-Issa (Ed.), *Gender and psychopathology* (pp. 3–29). New York: Academic Press.

Barraclough, B. M. (1971). Suicide in the elderly. In D. W. Kay & A. Walk (Eds.), *Recent developments in psychogeriatrics* (pp. 87–97). Ashford, England: Hedley Brothers.

Benson, R. A., & Brodie, D. C. (1975). Suicide by overdose of medicines among the aged. *Journal of the American Geriatrics Society, 23*, 304–308.

Bock, E. W. (1972). Aging and suicide: The significance of marital, kinship, and alternative relations. *The Family Coordinator, 21*, 71–79.

Bock, E. W., & Webber, I. L. (1972). Social status and the relational system of elderly suicides: A reexamination of the Henry-Short thesis. *Life-Threatening Behavior, 2*, 145–159.

Breed, W., & Huffine, C. L. (1979). Sex differences in suicide among older white Americans: A role and developmental approach. In C. J. Kaplan (Ed.), *Psychopathology of aging* (pp. 289–309). New York: Academic Press.

Canetto, S. S. (1991). Gender roles, suicide attempts and substance abuse. *Journal of Psychology, 125*, 605–620.

Cath, S. H. (1980). Suicide in the middle years: Some reflections on the annihilation of the self. In W. H. Norman & T. J. Scaramella (Eds.), *Mid-life: Developmental and clinical issues* (pp. 53–72). New York: Brunner/Mazel.

Chesler, P. (1972). *Women and madness*. New York: Doubleday.

Conwell, Y., Rotenberg, M., & Caine, E. D. (1990). Completed suicide at age 50 and over. *Journal of the American Geriatric Society, 38*, 640–644.

Cumming, E., & Lazar, C. (1981). Kinship structure and suicide: A theoretical link. *Canadian Review of Sociology and Anthropology, 18*, 271–281.

Davis, J. C. (1904). Suicide with some illustrative cases. *Journal of the American Medical Association, 43*, 212–123.

Diggory, J. C. (1976). United States suicide rates, 1922-1968: An analysis of some trends. In E. S. Shneidman (Ed.), *Suicidology: Contemporary developments* (pp. 30–69). New York: Grune & Stratton.

Dublin, L. (1963). *Suicide: A sociological and statistical study.* New York: Ronald Press.

Durkheim, E. (1951). *Suicide* (J. A. Spaulding & G. Simpson, Trans.). Glencoe, IL: Free Press (Original work published 1897).

Essa, M., & Howell-Burke, D. (1984). Toward reducing the morbidity and mortality of the elderly bereaved. *Nebraska Medical Journal, 69,* 272–274.

Farberow, N. L., & Shneidman, E. S. (1957). Suicide and age. In E. S. Shneidman & N. L. Farberow (Eds.), *Clues to suicide* (pp. 41–49). New York: McGraw Hill.

Furst, S. S., & Ostow, M. (1979). The psychodynamics of suicide. In L. D. Hankoff & B. Einsidler (Eds.), *Suicide: Theory and clinical aspects* (pp. 165–178). Littleton, MA: PSG Publishing.

Gardner, E. A., Bahn, A. K., & Mack, M. (1964). Suicide and psychiatric care in the aging. *Archives of General Psychiatry, 10,* 547–553.

George, L. K. (1990). Gender, age and psychiatric disorders. *Generations, 14,* 22–27.

Gove, W. R. (1972). Sex, marital status and suicide. *Journal of Health and Social Behavior, 13,* 204–213.

Hess, B. H. (1990). The demographic parameters of gender and aging. *Generations, 14,* 12–16.

Holinger, P. C. (1987). *Violent deaths in the United States.* New York: Guilford.

Holt, L., & Datan, N. (1984). Senescence, sex roles, and stress: Shepherding resources into old age. In C. S. Widom (Ed.), *Sex roles and psychopathology* (pp. 339–352). New York: Plenum Press.

Jarvis, J. K., Ferrence, R. G., Johnson, F. G., & Whitehead, P. C. (1976). Sex and age patterns in self-injury. *Journal of Health and Social Behavior, 17,* 145–154.

Kaplan, A. G., & Klein, R. B. (1989). Women and suicide. In D. J. Jacobs & H. N. Brown (Eds.), *Suicide: Understanding and responding* (pp. 257–282). Madison, CT: International Universities Press.

Kirsling, R. A. (1986). Review of suicide among elderly persons. *Psychological Reports, 59,* 359–366.

Kushner, H. I. (1985). Women and suicide in historical perspective. *Signs: Journal of Women in Culture and Society, 10,* 537–552.

Lester, D. (1969). Suicidal behavior in men and women. *Mental Hygiene, 53,* 340–345.

Lester, D. (1972). *Why people kill themselves.* Springfield, IL: Thomas.

Lester, D. (1979). Sex differences in suicidal behavior. In E. S. Gomberg & V. Franks (Eds.), *Gender and disordered behavior* (pp. 287–300). New York: Brunner/Mazel.

Lester, D. (1988). Suicide and the menstrual cycle. In D. Lester (Ed.), *Why women kill themselves* (pp. 111–118). Springfield, IL: Thomas.

Lester, D. (1989). The study of suicide from a feminist perspective. *Crisis, 11,* 38–43.

Levenson, M. (1974). Cognitive correlates of suicidal risk. In C. Neuringer (Ed.), *Psychological assessment of suicidal risk* (pp. 150–163). Springfield, IL: Thomas.

Linehan, M. M. (1971). Toward a theory of sex differences in suicidal behavior. *Crisis Intervention, 3,* 93–101.

Linehan, M. M. (1973). Suicide and attempted suicide: Study of perceived sex differences. *Perceptual and Motor Skills, 37,* 31–34.

Lyons, M. J. (1984). Suicide in later life: Some putative causes with implications for prevention. *Journal of Community Psychology, 12,* 379–388.

MacMahon, B., & Pugh, T. F. (1965). Suicide in the widowed. *American Journal of Epidemiology, 81,* 23–31.

Manton, K. G., Blazer, D. G., & Woodbury, M. A. (1987). Suicide in middle age and later life: Sex and race specific life table and cohort analyses. *Journal of Gerontology, 42,* 219–227.

Marks, A., & Abernathy, T. (1974). Toward a sociocultural perspective on means of self-destruction. *Suicide & Life-Threatening Behavior, 4,* 3–17.

Marks, A., & Stokes, C. S. (1976). Socialization, firearms and suicide. *Social Problems, 5,* 622–639.

McClure, G. M. G. (1987). Suicide in England and Wales, 1975-1984, *British Journal of Psychiatry, 150,* 309–314.

McIntosh, J. L. (1989). Official U.S. elderly suicide data bases: Levels, availability, omissions. *Omega, 19,* 337–350.

McIntosh, J. L., & Santos, J. F. (1986). Methods of suicide by age: Sex and age differences among the young and old. *International Journal of Aging and Human Development, 22,* 123–139.

Miller, H. L., Coombs, D. W., Leeper, J. D., & Barton, S. N. (1984). An analysis on the effects of suicide prevention facilities on suicide rates in the United States. *American Journal of Public Health, 74,* 340–343.

Miller, M. (1978). Geriatric suicide: The Arizona study. *The Gerontologist, 18,* 488–495.

Neuringer, C. (1982). Suicidal behavior in women. *Crisis, 3,* 41–49.

Neuringer, C., & Lettieri, D. J. (1982). *Suicidal women.* New York: Gardner Press.

Neuringer, C., Levenson, M., & Kaplan, J. M. (1971). Phenomenological time flow in suicidal, geriatric and normal individuals. *Omega, 2,* 247–251.

Osgood, N. J. (1985). *Suicide in the elderly.* Rockville, MD: Aspen.

Pierce, D. (1987). Deliberate self-harm in the elderly. *International Journal of Geriatric Psychiatry, 2,* 105–110.

Sainsbury, P. (1962). Suicide in late life. *Gerontologia Clinica, 4,* 161–170.

Sainsbury, P. (1963). Social and epidemiological aspects of suicide with special reference to the aged. In R. H. Williams, C. Tibbits, & W. Donahue (Eds.), *Processes of aging: Social and psychological perspectives* (Vol. 2, pp. 153–175). New York: Atherton.

Showalter, E. (1985). *The female malady: Women, madness and English culture, 1830–1980.* New York: Penguin.

Smith, D. W. E. (1990). The biology of gender and aging. *Generations, 14,* 7–11.

Stengel, E. (1964). *Suicide and attempted suicide.* Harmondworth, England: Penguin.

Stenback, A. (1980). Depression and suicidal behavior in old age. In J. E. Birren & B. Sloane (Eds.), *Handbook of mental health and aging* (pp. 616–652). Englewood Cliffs, NJ: Prentice-Hall.

Stillion, J. M., White, H., Edwards, P. J., & McDowell, E. E. (1989). Ageism and sexism in suicide attitudes. *Death Studies, 13,* 247–261.

Suter, B. (1976). Suicide and women. In B. B. Wolman & K. H. Krauss (Eds.), *Between survival and suicide* (pp. 129–161). New York: Gardner Press.

Troll, L. E., & Turner, B. F. (1979). Sex differences in problems of aging. In E. S. Gomberg & V. Franks (Eds.), *Gender and disordered behavior* (pp. 124–156). New York: Brunner/Mazel.

Victoroff, V. M. (1984). Depression in the elderly. *The Ohio State Medical Journal, 80,* 180–187.

Weissman, M. M., & Klerman, G. L. (1977). Sex differences and the epidemiology of depression. *Archives of General Psychiatry, 34,* 98–111.

White, H., & Stillion, J. M. (1988). Sex differences in attitudes toward suicide: Do males stigmatize males? *Psychology of Women Quarterly, 12,* 357–272.

Wilson, M. (1981). Suicidal behavior: Toward an explanation of differences in female and male rates. *Suicide & Life-Threatening Behavior, 11,* 131–139.

Zarit, S. H. (1980). *Aging and mental disorders: Psychological approaches to assessment and treatment.* New York: Free Press.

7

Environmental Factors in Suicide in Long-Term Care Facilities

Nancy J. Osgood, PhD
Virginia Commonwealth University/Medical College of Virginia

ABSTRACT: One major purpose of this study was to identify environmental factors related to suicide in long-term care facilities. Questionnaires were mailed to a random sample of administrators at 1,080 facilities. Information was collected on facility characteristics, overt suicide, and intentional life-threatening behavior.

Chi-square analyses revealed 4 environmental characteristics related to suicidal behavior and deaths from suicide: staff turnover, size, auspices, and per diem cost. More suicides occurred in larger facilities and facilities with higher staff turnover. Religious or "other" facilities experienced more suicidal deaths than public or private facilities; facilities charging less experienced more deaths.

There are approximately 23,000 long-term care facilities serving over 2.5 million elderly in the United States today. The average number of elderly in nursing homes is expected to increase 76% between now and the year 2020. The prevention of suicide and other forms of self-destructive behavior among the institutionalized elderly is a major consideration because of its importance from the humanitarian, professional, and legal points of view.

To date, little research on overt suicide among elderly residents of long-term care facilities has been conducted. Overt suicide includes wrist slashing, jumping, hanging, asphyxiation, and shooting. Similarly, few studies have examined the problem of what has been referred to as "indirect life-threatening behavior" by Nelson and Farberow (1980). Indirect life-threatening behavior (ILTB) is defined as repetitive acts

Funds for this study were provided by the Virginia Commonwealth University Grant-in-Aid to faculty. A more comprehensive version of this paper was presented at the annual meeting of the American Association of Suicidology, Washington, DC on April 16, 1988.

by individuals directed toward themselves that result in physical harm or tissue damage that could bring about a premature end of life. Examples include: refusing to eat or drink, refusing medication, or refusing to follow specified medical regimens.

One study conducted on the geriatric ward of a Veterans Administration Medical Center (Wolff, 1970) suggests that overt suicide does occur in long-term care facilities. Other studies have also revealed a fairly high incidence of ILTB in particular long-term care facilities studied (Mishara & Kastenbaum, 1973; Nelson, 1977; Nelson & Farberow, 1980).

The institutionalized elderly, who are the more vulnerable than other elderly persons due to functional deficits and lack of other social support, are also more dependent on their immediate environment (George, 1980) and often are able to exercise less control over their environments and activities. Frequently, staff overindulgence and overprotection and personal loss of control in the immediate environment can evoke feelings of uselessness, personal inadequacy, a sense of dependency, helplessness, and depression. Factors such as these can place the older person at risk for overt or intentional life-threatening suicidal behavior. We currently have very limited knowledge of the impact of environment on suicidal behavior. One major purpose of the present study was to identify environmental factors related to suicide in long-term care facilities.

Review of Literature

A significant body of literature that identifies environmental factors that affect quality of life and/or patient outcomes (morbidity, mortality, happiness) in long-term care facilities currently exists. Size, facility ownership or auspices, cost, and staff turnover rate have been identified as environmental factors that significantly influence quality of care and/or patient outcomes.

The early work of Greenwald and Linn (1971) suggests that as homes for the aged increase in size, patient satisfaction, activity, and communication decline. In a study of licensed homes in Ohio, Curry and Ratliff (1973) found that residents in smaller facilities were less isolated, developed more relationships and contacts within the home, had relative visits at least monthly, and overall, were more sociable than were residents of larger facilities. More recently, researchers who have examined the role of privacy, a factor directly related to size of facility, have emphasized the importance of privacy to resident well-being (Tate, 1980; Louis, 1983). Among elderly in institutions, the most private space known to them is their room (Koncelik, 1979). Privacy is essential to maintaining positive self-regard and personal autonomy and to providing emotional release. Larger facilities with more residents offer less privacy to older individuals.

Per diem cost has also been shown to influence quality of care. Greenwald and Linn (1971) found a direct relationship between quality of care and cost, with higher cost facilities providing higher quality of care. Ullman (1984) found that facilities charging higher per diem rates provided better quality care. The more expensive facilities provided better quality staff and more and better quality therapies and services than did those facilities charging less.

One recent study of turnover in long-term care facilities (Halbur, 1986) documented staff turnover rates between 55% and 75% in several states. In their analysis of secondary data, Wallace and Brubaker (1984) found turnover rates from 50% to 150%. A large body of literature currently exists on the negative effects of high staff turnover on patient morale, quality of care, and other outcomes (Kohn & Biache, 1982; Kane, Hammer, & Byrnes, 1977; Knapp & Harissis, 1981). Personnel in long-term care facilities fill the roles of caretakers and, often, as friends of residents (Stryker-Gordon, 1979). It becomes difficult to adequately achieve quality of care in a constantly changing environment that requires residents to adjust to new faces in old places. It is equally as difficult for residents to begin to know and trust staff members when they leave so frequently. Negative treatment outcomes resulting from the impact of staff turnover are entirely possible and probable.

Study Design and Method

For this study, a national random sample of 1,080 institutions was computer-generated from the National Master Facility Inventory obtained from the Long-Term Care Statistics Branch of the National Center for Health Statistics. A detailed, written questionnaire and consent form were mailed to administrators of each facility. The questionnaire included items on the facility (size, location, ownership, cost, etc.), staff and residents (staff/patient ratio, staff turnover rate, etc.), and items on the number of overt suicides, suicide attempts, incidents of ILTB, and deaths from ILTB during 1984 and 1985. The questionnaire was pretested and adjusted before the initial mailing. One telephone follow-up and two mail follow-ups resulted in the return of 463 (43%) completed questionnaires from administrators in all regions of the country. Further details of the methods of this investigation may be found in the book, *Suicide Among the Elderly in Long-Term Care Facilities* (Osgood, Brant, & Lipman, 1991).

Facilities differed in size (from less than 10 beds to more than 100 beds), setting (urban to small town), sponsorship/ownership (public to fraternal), cost (from under $20 a day to over $100), rate of staff turnover (from under 10% a year to over 50% a year), staff to patient ratio (from 5 patients for each staff member to over 11 patients per staff member), and type or level of care (skilled to domiciliary and other care types/ levels). Table 1 provides an overview of characteristics of the 463 facilities included in the study.

The total resident population consisted of 30,269 residents. Residents ranged in age from 22 to 91, with a mean age of 65 years. Seventy-eight percent of the residents were over 65 years of age, 16% were aged 40 to 65 years, and 6% were under 40. Seventy-four percent of the residents were caucasian, while 7% were non-caucasian.

Data Analysis and Findings

Chi-square techniques were used to test whether or not any facility characteristic, such as size or per diem cost, significantly determined whether suicidal behaviors occurred in the institution and whether deaths from suicide occurred. Facilities that reported some suicidal behavior were compared to facilities that reported none. Facilities that reported some deaths from suicide were compared with facilities that reported none.

Chi-square analyses revealed two environmental characteristics related to suicide. Each made a significant difference in whether or not any incidents of suicidal behavior were experienced. Staff turnover and size of facility (number of residents) were important predictors of suicidal behavior. Those facilities experiencing a high turnover in staff were much more likely to experience some form of suicidal behavior (overt or ILTB) than were those facilities with low staff turnover ($\chi^2 = 23.04$, df = 3, $p = < .001$).

Ninety percent of those facilities that had a staff turnover rate of less than 10% per year experienced no suicidal behavior, and 10% experienced some instances of such behavior. By contrast, in facilities experiencing staff turnover of 50% or greater, 75% reported no suicidal behaviors and 26% reported some behaviors. Results of the analyses are displayed in Table 2.

Size of resident population was the other facility characteristic associated with suicidal behaviors in the institution. Largely populated facilities were significantly more likely to have some incidence of suicidal behavior (overt or ILTB) than were small facilities ($\chi^2 = 8.62$, df = 3, $p = < .05$). Of those facilities with under 10 residents, only 7% experienced

TABLE 1. Characteristics of Facilities

Characteristics	N	% of total
Region of the Country		
New England	30	7.00
Mid-Atlantic	44	10.00
South Atlantic	77	18.00
East South Central	20	4.00
East North Central	89	20.00
West South Central	27	6.00
West North Central	60	13.00
Mountain	17	4.00
Pacific	84	19.00
No Response	15	
TOTAL	463	100.00[a]
Facility Setting		
Urban	136	30.00
Suburban	112	24.00
Rural	193	42.00
Small Town	14	3.00
Other	3	
No Response	5	
TOTAL	463	100.00[a]
Facility Size (No. of Residents)		
Under 10	76	16.00
10–50	154	33.00
51–100	134	29.00
100+	99	21.00
TOTAL	463	100.00[a]
Turnover by Facilities Per Year		
Up to 10%	209	45.00
11–25%	52	11.00
25–50%	66	14.00
Over 50%	136	29.00
TOTAL	463	100.00[a]
Sponsorship/Ownership		
Public (federal, state, local)	85	19.00
Private	176	39.00
Proprietary	131	29.00
Religious	51	11.00
Fraternal	3	
Other	11	1.00
No Response	6	
TOTAL	463	100.00[a]
Bed Certification		
Skilled Care	105	24.00
Intermediate Care	169	39.00
Swing	9	2.00
Adult Home	100	23.00
Domiciliary Care[b]	22	5.00
Other	32	7.00
No Response	26	
TOTAL	463	100.00[a]
Per Diem Charge		
Under $20	62	15.00
$21–49	183	44.00
$50–100	116	28.00
Over $100	56	13.00
No Response	46	
TOTAL	463	100.00[a]
Staff to Patient Ratio (All direct-care staff)		
Less than 1:5	286	77.00
1:5 to 1:8	43	12.00
1:8 to 1:10	13	4.00
1:11 or more	28	8.00
No Response	93	
TOTAL	463	100.00[a]

[a] Rounded
[b] Called bed and board homes in some states

TABLE 2.   Annual Staff Turnover and Total Suicides

	Suicides			
	None		Some	
Annual Staff Turnover	N	$\%^a$	N	$\%^a$
Up to 10%	189	50	20	24
11%–25%	35	9	17	20
25%–50%	54	14	12	14
Over 50%	101	27	35	42
Total	379	82	84	18
No responses (0)				

Total n = 463 χ^2 = 23.04, df = 3, p = < .001.
^{a} Rounded number

any suicidal behavior—compared to facilities with over 100 residents, of which 22% experienced some suicidal behaviors. Results of the analyses are displayed in Table 3.

Two other facility characteristics were significantly related to whether or not residents died from engaging in suicidal acts. Per diem cost and auspices (public, private, religious, other) were both important. Death from suicide (overt or ILTB) was much less frequent in high-cost facilities than in those that charged less for their services (χ^2 = 8.02, df = 3, p = < .05). Facilities that charged over $100 per day, the most expensive institutions, reported no deaths from suicide. By comparison, of those facilities charging less than $20 per day, 4% experienced some deaths from suicide. Of those facilities charging $20 to $49 per day, 9% experienced some deaths from suicidal behavior. Results of the analyses are displayed in Table 4.

TABLE 3.   Size of Resident Population and Total
Suicidal Behaviors

	Suicidal Behaviors			
	None		Some	
Number of Residents	N	$\%^a$	N	$\%^a$
Under 10	70	19	5	6
11–49	121	32	33	39
50–100	109	29	25	30
Over 100	78	20	21	25
Total	378	82	84	18
No responses (0)				

Total n = 463 χ^2 = 8.615, df = 3, p = < .05
^{a} Rounded number

TABLE 4.   Per Diem Cost and Total Number
of Deaths by Suicide

| Cost Per Day | Deaths by Suicide | | | |
| | None | | Some | |
	N	$\%^a$	N	$\%^a$
Under $20	60	16	2	7
$20–49	168	43	15	52
$50–100	104	27	12	41
Over $100	56	14	0	0
Total	388	93	29	7
No responses (46)				

Total $n = 463$ $\chi^2 = 8.015$, df $= 3$, $p = < .05$
^{a} Rounded number

The type of facility or auspice under which the institution is managed was also a factor in whether or not deaths occurred from suicide. Public and private facilities experienced significantly fewer deaths than did religious or "other" facilities ($\chi^2 = 7.14$, df $= 3$, $p = < .10$). Results of the analyses are displayed in Table 5.

Summary and Discussion

This study represents the first major large-scale study of suicide in long-term facilities in the United States. Results of this study revealed four environmental characteristics related to occurrence of suicidal behavior and death from suicide in such facilities: size, auspices, per

TABLE 5.   Type of Auspice and Total Deaths
by Suicide (Overt and ILTB Died)

| Auspice | Deaths by Suicide | | | |
| | None | | Some | |
	N	$\%^a$	N	$\%^a$
Public	79	19	6	20
Private	171	40	5	17
Religious	46	11	5	17
Other	427	93	30	7
Total	131	31	14	47
No responses (6)				

Total $n = 463$ $\chi^2 = 7.143$, df $= 3$, $p = < .10$
^{a} Rounded number

diem cost, and staff turnover rate. These same characteristics have previously been shown to affect quality of care and patient outcomes in general.

Findings must be interpreted with caution in light of the limitations of the study. Suicide is a very sensitive subject to investigate; therefore, data reported by administrators may not have been complete or totally accurate. Basically, analyses were descriptive. We were unable to analyze data using multivariate techniques. Many of the 463 facilities reported no suicidal behaviors and no deaths from suicide; thus a multiple regression analysis of the differential impact of different environmental factors in suicide was not appropriate. Therefore, it is impossible to identify the relative importance of each environmental factor to variation in suicide. Future studies utilizing much larger samples of facilities and employing measures to assure more accurate reporting of suicide should be conducted to provide the data base necessary to perform multivariate analyses to determine the relative impact of various environmental factors on overt suicide and ILTB in institutions.

Keeping these limitations in mind, we were still able to identify four environmental factors related to suicide. This information can aid in suicide prevention and promotion of mental health among residents. Knowledge regarding particular environmental factors that encourage suicide among elderly residents can be incorporated into staff education and training. Modifications of existing facilities and plans for future facilities, based on the results of this study, could minimize the incidence of suicidal behaviors among the institutionalized elderly. Designing smaller facilities or modifying larger ones to accommodate the resident's need for personal space, privacy, autonomy, and individuality could potentially reduce suicide. So could measures aimed at retaining staff, particularly through better pay, improved working conditions, more fringe benefits, better staff training, and development of feelings of loyalty and belonging in workers. Since higher-cost facilities are less likely to experience deaths from suicide, as reported by administrators, perhaps incorporating some of the services, staff characteristics, and other relevant features of such facilities into other facilities would prove beneficial in reducing deaths from suicide in the nursing home population.

These suggestions represent only a few that could be offered. The important point from this study, as pointed out earlier by Kiernat (1983), is that environment is such an important factor in the health and overall well-being of individuals that it represents "the hidden modality" in rehabilitation programs. Modifying the institutional environment could be a major measure in suicide prevention in long-term care institutions.

References

Curry, T. J., & Ratliff, B. W. (1973). The effects of nursing home size on resident isolation and life satisfaction: Part I. *Gerontologist, 13*(3), 295–298.

Elwell, F. (1984). The effects of ownership on institutional services. *Gerontologist, 24*(1), 77–83.

George, L. K. (1980). *Role transitions in later life.* Monterey, CA: Brooks/Cole.

Greenwald, S. R., & Linn, M. W. (1971). Intercorrelation of data on nursing homes. *Gerontologist, 11*, 337–340.

Halbur, B. (1986). Managing nursing personnel turnover rates. *The Journal of Applied Gerontology, 5*(1), 64–75.

Kane, R., Hammer, D., & Byrnes, N. (1977). Getting care to nursing home patients: A problem and a proposal. *Medical Care, 15*, 174–180.

Kiernat, J. M. (1983). Environment: The hidden modality. *Physical and Occupational Therapy in Geriatrics, 2*(1), 3–12.

Knapp, M., & Harissis, K. (1981). Staff vacancies and turnover in British people's homes. *Gerontologist, 21*, 76–84.

Kohn, G. L., & Biache, A. S. (1982). Developing a career ladder for nursing personnel. *The Journal of Long-Term Care Administration, 10*, 25–27.

Koncelik, J. A. (1979). Human factors and environmental design for the aging: Physiological change in sensory loss as design criteria. In T. O. Byerts, S. C. Howell, & L. A. Pastalan (Eds.), *Environmental context of aging.* NY: Garland.

Louis, M. (1983). Personal space boundary needs of elderly persons: An empirical study. *Journal of Gerontological Nursing, 7*(7), 395–400.

Mishara, B., & Kastenbaum, R. (1973). Self-injurious behavior and environmental change in the institutionalized elderly. *International Journal of Aging and Human Development, 4*, 133–145.

Nelson, F. L. (1977). Religiosity and self-destructive crises in the institutionalized elderly. *Suicide & Life-Threatening Behavior, 7*, 67–74.

Nelson, F. L., & Farberow, N. L. (1980). Indirect self-destructive behavior in the elderly nursing home patient. *Journal of Gerontology, 35*, 949–957.

Osgood, N. J., Brant, B. A., & Lipman, A. (1991). *Suicide among the elderly in long-term care facilities.* Westport, CT: Greenwood.

Stryker-Gordon, R. (1979). Minnesota study suggests means of reducing turnover rates in nursing homes. *Journal of Nursing Administration, 9*(4), 17–20.

Tate, J. W. (1980). The need for personal space in institutions for the elderly. *Journal of Applied Gerontology, 6*, 139–148.

Ullman, S. (1984). Ownership, costs, and facility characteristics in the national long-term health care industry. *Journal of Applied Gerontology, 3*, 43–49.

Wallace, R., & Brubaker, T. (1984). Long-term care with short-term workers: An examination of nursing home aide turnover. *Journal of Applied Gerontology, 3*(1), 50–58.

Wolff, K. (1970). Observations of depression and suicide in the geriatric patient. In K. Wolff (Ed.), *Patterns of self-destruction: Depression and suicide* (pp. 86–95). Illinois: Charles C. Thomas.

8

The Role of Social Supports in the Bereavement Process of Surviving Spouses of Suicide and Natural Deaths

Norman L. Farberow
Los Angeles Suicide Prevention Center
Dolores Gallagher-Thompson
Stanford University
VA Medical Center
Michael Gilewski
Physical Medicine and Rehabilitation
Cedars-Sinai Medical Center
Larry Thompson
Stanford University
VA Medical Center

ABSTRACT: This report examines the changing role of social supports in the bereavement of spouses of elderly suicide and natural deaths, focusing on differences and similarities in relation to gender, time, and mode of death. Measurements were obtained 4 times after death (within 2 months, at 6 months, at 12 months, and at 2 to 2½ years) on 79% of the 108 survivors of elderly suicide, 89% of the 199 natural death survivors, and 79% of the nonbereaved controls. The results indicated that the suicide survivors received significantly less emotional support for their feelings of depression and grief than the natural death survivors, and that they did not confide in the persons in their network any more than the nonbereaved controls did. Women report receiving more support overall than men. A low spot in social supports occurred at the 6-month point after loss for both bereaved groups, but primarily in practical help received by natural death survivors. By the end of the second year, both practical and emotional supports had increased to at least the same level as immediately after death.

This research was supported by Grants Nos. R01-MH3684 from the National Institute of Mental Health and R01-AG01959 from the National Institute on Aging.

The death of a spouse was considered by Holmes and Rahe (1967) to be one of the most difficult stressful events in the experience of adults, with impact on the spouse survivor physically, economically, emotionally, and socially (Antonovsky, 1979; Cain & Fast, 1966; Parkes, 1985; Schuchter & Zisook, 1986). Social support has been recognized by researchers and theorists in the field of bereavement as an important factor in the process of adaptation to loss and recovery of function, identity, and status (Osterweis, Solomon, & Green, 1984; Dimond, Lund, & Caserta, 1987; Bankoff, 1983). The process of adaptation to such a loss requires formation of new identities (Averill, 1968; Lopata, 1973; Saunders, 1981). The development of new social attachments and reorganization of old relationships (Raphael, 1983; Gallagher, Breckenridge, Thompson, & Peterson, 1983; Glick, Parkes, & Weiss, 1975).

While most of the earlier studies were conducted on adult populations covering all ages, several researchers in recent years have focused on the elderly, generally aged 55 and older (Heyman & Gianturco, 1973; Lund, Caserta, & Dimond, 1986). In recent years, bereavement among the elderly has begun to receive considerable attention. Lund's book, *Older Bereaved Spouses* (1989), for example, reports on research with practical applications and draws a number of generalizations from the nine studies that make up the book. The conclusions are significant: bereavement adjustments are multidimensional, with nearly every aspect of a person's life affected; while bereavement is stressful, many older surviving spouses are quite resilient; the overall impact of bereavement on the physical and mental health of many older spouses is not so devastating as expected; and loneliness and problems associated with the tasks of daily living are two of the most common and difficult adjustments for older bereaved persons.

For the past several years, we have been conducting a comprehensive study evaluating the process of adaptation in the course of bereavement of elderly survivors of suicide. They have been studied longitudinally over a 2½ year period after their spouse's death, noting especially the impact on emotional and physical health, the course of grief, and the roles of social support, coping strengths, and cumulative losses and stresses on adaptation. Previous papers have reported on the early impact of bereavement on psychological distress in the spouse–survivors (Farberow, Gallagher, Gilewski, & Thompson, 1987), the interaction of depression and bereavement on mental health (Gilewski, Farberow, Gallagher, & Thompson, 1991), and long-term mental health, grief, and personality changes in the bereavement of spouses of elderly suicides and natural deaths (Farberow, Gallagher, Gilewski, & Thompson, 1991). This report focuses on the changing role of social supports in the bereavement of spouses of older adults and examines differences in terms of gender, time, and mode of death. To our knowledge, it is the first study to examine this combination of factors in a large urban sample.

Method

Details of precedure, methodology, and selection of population samples are provided in previous papers. Briefly summarized, data were collected on 3 groups: (1) 110 survivors of elderly suicides (SS, 88 women and 22 men); (2) 199 natural death survivors (NDS, 95 men and 104 women); and (3) 163 nonbereaved controls (NBC, 78 women and 85 men) who were obtained from senior centers, residential facilities for elders, or from volunteer groups at local universities. Criteria for inclusion among controls were being currently married and not having lost a spouse within the last 5 years. All subjects were age 55 years or older ($M = 67.55$, $SD = 8.39$), caucasian, and predominantly females (370 women and 202 men).

Measurements were obtained at 4 times after death: T_1 was within 2 months; T_2 was 6 months after death; T_3 was 12 months after the death; and T_4 was between 24 and 30 months post-loss. Measures obtained included both a structured interview (inquiring about such topics as additional losses experienced since the spouse's death, nature of coping strategies used, extent and adequacy of the social support network, how the respondent felt he or she was coping in general, quality of the marital relationship, self-reported physical health problems, and others) and a variety of self-report questionnaires (not reported on here) designed to measure grief, depression, and other symptoms of distress. Respondents with complete data for the full 2½ year study consisted of 71% of the original suicide group, 89% of the natural death group, and 79% of the comparison control group sampled at the beginning of the study. Most of our participants were from a lower-middle income level with an average of at least a high school education. When the groups were found to differ on some of the demographic characteristics, the background variables were summarized in four principal components: spouse's socioeconomic status, longevity, respondent's socioeconomic status, and respondent's income. In addition, the four component factor scores were used as covariates in the analyses.

Data were analyzed evaluating the significance of changes over time by means of Multivariate Analyses of Variance (MANOVAs) with repeated measures both between and within subjects. Significance levels were denoted by Wilk's lambda. Linear and curvilinear patterns indicated consistent patterns of increase and decrease over time, and a U, inverted U, or wave pattern throughout the four time periods. Univariate analyses of variance (ANOVAs) were then conducted where categories were significant, and Newman-Keuls tests were applied using the composite mean scores for each variable at each time for each group, with adjustments for covariates in order to determine exactly which groups differed from each other.

Construction of Composite Indices of Social Support

Data were obtained on several critical areas of support based upon our review of the then-extant literature. The large number of variables in each of the major areas made it desirable to reduce the data by construction of indices. Variables relating to distinct areas of support were categorized, resulting in the construction of nine social support indices:

1. *Practical help received.* Six items evaluated the help received (rated 1–7 for completely, through somewhat, to not at all) with money problems, discharging financial responsibilities, transportation, conducting housework, obtaining household and car repairs, and finding legal and insurance aid.

2. *Interpersonal/emotional help.* Three items evaluated the help received (rated 1–7 from completely, through somewhat, to not at all) in combating emotional problems of depression and discouragement, and obtaining companionship both inside and outside of the home.

3. *Number of supporting people.* One item asked for the number of important people the survivors were currently in contact with in person, by letter, and by telephone. These people were added, to comprise the total number in the survivors' social support network.

4. *Frequency of contacts with the people in the current network* (rated 1–7 from every day through less than every 2–3 months).

5. *Level of feelings for persons in the current network* (rated 1–7 for very positive, through neutral, through very negative).

6. *Level of confiding in persons in the current network* (rated from completely, to somewhat, to not at all).

The next three indices consisted of averages for the last three items above.

7. *Average number of contacts with persons in their network.*

8. *Average level of feelings for persons in network.*

9. *Average degree of confiding in persons in network.*

Results

Between Groups Measures

Multivariate measures yielded significant main effects for group, $F(18,268) = 2.20$, $p < .004$, and sex $F(9,134) = 2.19$, $p < .026$. Effects for group by sex were not significant.

Univariate measures between groups were significant for 5 of the 9 indices (df = 2,142 for each): practical help received, $p < .019$; emotional help, $p < .020$; frequency of contacts with people in the network, $p < .015$; level of feelings for people in the network, $p < .006$; and level of confiding in network people, $p < .030$ (see Table 1).

Table 2 presents the results of Newman-Keuls tests comparing cumulative means between groups. These data indicate that over 2 years of bereavement, the NDS received significantly more practical help than the NBC, but not more than the SS. The SS were not significantly differentiated from either group. The NDS received significantly more emotional help than the SS, but not more than the NBC. The NBC were not significantly differentiated from either bereaved group. The SS had significantly less frequency of contact with network people than the NBC but not significantly less than the NDS. The NDS had significantly more positive feelings for the people in their network and confided in them more deeply than the NBC. Finally, the SS were not significantly different from the other two groups on either index.

Univariate measure for sex yielded significant effects for 3 indices (df = 1,142 for each) with Newman-Keuls indicating that females more than males rated themselves as receiving more practical help, $p < .001$; having more people in their current network, $p < .033$; and feeling more positively about the people in their network, $p < .025$ (see Table 1 for significant univariate measures and Table 2 for cumulative cell means).

Within Group Measures

Multivariate measures within groups for changes over time were computed for linear, quadratic, and cubic effects. Where significant effects were obtained, univariate measures were computed within categories and Newman-Keuls tests were used to determine the significance of indicated differences.

TABLE 1. Significant Univariate Effects of Social Support Indices Between and Within Groups of Survivors of Elderly Natural Deaths, Suicides, and NonBereaved Controls

	Between		Within					
			Linear			Quadratic		Cubic
Indices	G	S	T	G × T	G × S × T	T	G × S × T	G × S × T
df	2,142	1,142	1,265	2,265	2,265	1,142	2,242	2,242
Help received								
Practical	4.08[a]	11.08[c]			3.04[a]	6.59[a]		
Emotional	4.02[a]		16.69[c]	7.17[c]	6.22[b]	9.95[b]		6.59[b]
No. important people in network		4.65[a]						
Primary support person								
Frequency of contact	4.30[a]		4.56[a]	3.88[a]				
Level of feelings for	5.34[b]	5.11[a]				5.58[a]	6.88[c]	3.29[a]
Degree of confiding	3.59[a]					8.45[b]		

Note: df = degrees of freedom; G = group; S = sex; T = time

[a] p < .05
[b] p < .01
[c] p < .001

TABLE 2. Cumulative and Cell Means of Significant Interactions of Social Support Indices Between Survivors of Elderly Natural Deaths, Elderly Suicides, and NonBereaved Controls

| | Cumulative means | | | | |
| | Group | | | Sex | |
Indices	NDS	NBC	SS	M	F
Help received					
Practical[b]	151.06	160.16	156.69	160.45	153.25
Emotional[a]	58.87	63.72	67.07		
No. important people in network				17.38	20.09
Primary support person					
Frequency of contact[c]	7.76	6.37	8.36		
Level of feelings for[b]	4.54	5.82	5.24	5.70	4.93
Degree of confiding[b]	7.94	9.74	8.64		

Note: The lower the value, the greater/more positive the degree of the index (except for number)
[a] Significant difference between NDS/SS
[b] Significant difference between NDS/NBC
[c] Significant difference between SS/NBC

Linear effects

MANCOVAs indicated significant effects for time, $F(9, 257) = 3.06$, $p < .002$; group by time, $F(18,514) = 2.04$, $p < .007$; and group by sex by time, $F(18,514) = 1.65$, $p < .0001$.

Univariate measures for time (df = 1,265) indicated significant effects for emotional help received, $p < .0001$, with an increase in the amount occurring over the 2-year period; and for the frequency of contact among the people in their network, $p < .034$, with the frequency of contacts increasing (see Table 1 for univariate measures and Table 3 for cumulative cell means).

Univariate measures for group by time (df = 2,265) yielded significant effects for emotional help received, $p < .001$, with the NDS reporting significantly more emotional help received across time than the NBC, and both groups more than the SS (see Table 3).

Significant effects were found for the frequency of contacts with persons in their network, $p < .022$, with the NBC reporting a significantly greater increase in contacts across the 2 years with the persons in their network than both the SS and the NDS (see Table 3).

Univariate measures for group by sex by time (df = 2,265) indicated significant effects for practical help received, $p < .050$, with males receiving more help over time than females among the NDS, and females receiving more help than males among the NBC and among the SS (see Table 3).

TABLE 3. Cumulative and Cell Means of Social Support Indices with Significant Linear Effects within Survivors of Elderly Natural Deaths, Elderly Suicides and NonBereaved Controls

		Linear Means					
			Group by time[a]			Group by sex by time		
Indices	Time	NDS	NBC	SS	NDS	NBC	SS
Practical help received							
Male					-1.64	-0.28	1.36
Female					0.14	-3.30	-0.03
Emotional help received[b]	-2.24	-3.65	-1.74	0.22			
Male					-5.96	-0.10	-0.09
Female					-2.33	-3.95	0.31
Frequency of contact with primary support person[c]	-.016	0.11	-0.56	0.00			

Note: Negative numbers reflect an increase toward the more positive end of the index
[a] Significant differences for group by time
[b] NBC v (NDS = SS)
[c] NDS v NBC v SS

Significant effects were also found for emotional help, $p < .002$, with males receiving more help than females in both the NDS and the SS, but less among the NBC (see Table 3).

Quadratic effects

MANCOVAs for quadratic effects within subjects were significant for effects of time, $F(9,134) = 3.78$, $p < .001$; and group by sex by time, $F(18,268) = 1.78$, $p < .027$. Effects for group by time and sex by time were not significant.

Univariate measures for time (df = 1,142) showed significant effects for practical help received, $p < .011$; emotional help received, $p < .002$; level of feelings toward persons in the network, $p < .020$; and degree of confiding in persons in the network, $p < .004$ (see Table 1).

The patterns for three of the four indices over time were similar, that is, a sharp lessening in the degree of practical help received, emotional help received, and degree of confiding in network appearing at T_2, 6 months after the loss. By T_3, 1 year after, each index had come back to or had even improved beyond the original level (at T_1). The index of level of feeling toward network persons showed no drop at T_2, but improved at T_3 and held at approximately the same level at T_4 (see Table 4). In general, a drop in the level of satisfaction with both practical and emotional help (also reflected in a drop in the level of confiding in network persons) appeared at the 6-month point in the bereavement period. However, these supports reappeared within the second 6 months and then either improved further or held throughout the second year. The level of feeling toward the network was the same for the first 6 months and then improved.

Univariate measures for group by sex by time (df = 2,142) indicated significant effects for the level of feelings toward the persons in the network, $p < .001$, for the SS only. Among this group, the females showed more positive levels of feeling than males throughout the first year toward the persons in their network, with the greatest gap at 1 year when males reported a considerable drop in the level of feelings toward their network, while women reported approximately the same level of feelings as at 6 months. By T_4, however, the males reported a marked improvement in the level of their feelings for their primary support person, while, for the females, the level of feelings lessened to about the same level it was within the first 4 weeks (see Table 4).

Cubic effects

MANCOVAs for cubic effects within subjects were significant for time, $F(9,134) = 2.03$, $p < .041$; and for group by sex by time, $F(18,268) = 1.72$, $p < .036$. Effects were not significant for group by time nor sex by time.

TABLE 4. Cumulative and Cell Means of Social Support Indices with Significant Quadratic Effects within Survivors of Elderly Natural Deaths, Elderly Suicides, and NonBereaved Controls

	Quadratic means[a]							
	Time				Group by sex by time			
Indices	T_1	T_2	T_3	T_4	T_1	T_2	T_3	T_4
Help received								
Practical	38.56	39.70	38.53	37.81				
Emotional	15.97	17.57	15.44	13.90				
Primary support person								
Level of feeling	1.37	1.37	1.27	1.30				
Suicide survivors								
Male					1.80	1.69	2.23	1.27
Female					1.40	1.12	1.15	1.35
Degree of confiding	2.04	2.54	2.08	2.10				

[a]The lower the value the more positive the degree of the index

Although cubic main effects were significant for time, exploration by univariate measurements revealed only trends toward significance among the nine indices and testing for differences was not carried out.

Univariate measurements for effects of group by sex by time (df = 2,142) were significant for emotional help received, $p < .002$, and for the level of feelings toward the persons in the network (see Table 1). In the latter, the results are the same as for the quadratic effects, with an increase in the level of feelings for females in the SS group in the first 6 months, then a return to the original level by T_4, after 2 years. For males, the level of feelings about persons in their network is poorest at 1 year, T_3, and markedly improved at 2 years, T_4 (see Table 5).

For the index of emotional help received, the pattern differed for the males and females in each bereaved group. Among the NDS, the males reported the same level for the first 6 months and then showed a marked increase in satisfaction both at 1 year and at 2 years. Females reported a marked decrease at T_2, but then the original level appeared at T_3, and there was even further improvement at T_4. Although females reported more help emotionally in the first month, by 6 months, T_2, there were practically no differences reported by males and females in the amount of emotional help received (see Table 5).

TABLE 5.   Cumulative and Cell Means of Social Support Indices with Significant Cubic Effects within Survivors of Elderly Natural Deaths, Elderly Suicides, and NonBereaved Controls

Indices	Cubic Means[a] Group by Sex by Time			
	T_1	T_2	T_3	T_4
Emotional help received				
NDS: Male	17.1	17.4	14.6	12.4
Female	15.2	17.4	14.7	12.7
NBC: Male	15.7	18.2	15.4	15.6
Female	16.5	18.0	16.0	13.0
SS: Male	15.6	17.9	17.4	16.5
Female	15.6	16.7	16.6	15.9
Level of feelings toward primary support person				
NDS: Male	1.28	1.23	1.30	1.21
Female	1.23	1.30	1.11	1.23
NBC: Male	1.45	1.68	1.37	1.37
Female	1.46	1.47	1.33	1.34
SS: Male	1.80	1.69	2.23	1.27
Female	1.40	1.12	1.15	1.35

[a] The lower the value the more positive the degree of the index

Among the SS, there was relatively little difference between males and females in the amount of emotional help received throughout the entire 2-year period. Both sexes reported less satisfaction from the emotional help received after the initial period, with the males reporting slightly less satisfaction than the females at every measurement point following (see Table 5).

Frequency of Support Relationships

Table 6 presents the frequency with which various relationships were mentioned spontaneously as being part of the individual's social network. It can be seen that for both bereaved groups, children were most often noted, irrespective of time of measurement, followed by close friends and siblings. In the nonbereaved comparison group (NBC), spouses, who, it should be remembered, were still alive and thus available, were more often mentioned than any other relative or friend, and this pattern remained true across time. There were no other significant differences among groups across time other than the relative importance of spouse versus children, as noted.

Discussion

In general, the results show that, from a social support standpoint, surviving the death of a spouse is more difficult when the death is a suicide than when the death is a natural one. Usually when such a loss occurs, there is a gathering around of the family, relatives, friends, and neighbors, offering condolences, sympathy, advice, emotional support, and much practical support. The survivors of suicide death in our study reported many differences in the degree to which such help was available. Thus, although there were no differences in the *number* of persons available for support for each of the bereaved groups during the 2 years after death occurred, there was a significant difference in the *amount* of emotional help received, with natural death survivors reporting experiencing more than suicide death survivors. While the latter group reported the less "positive" score on each of the other aspects of support, the differences were not significant, indicating that, in general, there were more similarities than differences between the two groups in the character and nature of the social supports they experienced during the first 2 years of their bereavement.

The above results seem directly related to those reported in our previous report on grief, mental health, and personality factors (Farberow

TABLE 6. Important People in the Social Network of Survivors of Elderly Natural Deaths, Elderly Suicides, and NonBereaved Controls

Percents[a]

Relationships Number	T$_1$ NDS 212	T$_1$ NBC 162	T$_1$ SS 108	T$_2$ NDS 164	T$_2$ NBC 148	T$_2$ SS 84	T$_3$ NDS 170	T$_3$ NBC 138	T$_3$ SS 75	T$_4$ NDS 144	T$_4$ NBC 123	T$_4$ SS 68
Child	67.5	30.1	63.0	59.1	23.8	56.0	59.4	21.7	52.0	57.6	8.9	61.8
Sibling	7.6	7.4	6.5	11.1	6.3	8.3	10.6	5.8	12.0	11.8	6.5	4.4
In-laws	3.8	1.0	0.0	2.4	0.0	0.0	1.8	1.0	1.3	2.1	0.0	1.5
Close friend	9.0	10.5	18.5	12.2	7.7	28.6	14.7	11.6	28.0	12.5	8.9	23.5
Spouse	0.5	45.1	0.0	1.0	55.9	0.0	4.1	52.2	1.3	7.6	70.7	1.5
Grandchild	1.4	1.0	1.0	4.3	0.0	1.2	2.9	1.4	2.7	2.1	0.0	2.9
Other relative	2.8	1.2	3.7	3.7	1.0	1.2	2.9	2.2	1.3	1.4	1.6	2.9

[a] Columns add to less than 100% because minimal relationships are omitted

et al., 1992). In that report it was noted that grief, severe depressive feelings, and general psychopathology took different courses for the two bereaved groups. The natural death survivors showed marked improvement in grief and depression at 6 months, while the suicide death survivors did not improve until after the first year. One might speculate that the greater emotional support experienced by the natural death survivors helped them to begin to recover earlier than the suicide death survivors. Lund (1989) points out in his studies that it is the qualitative dimensions of the network, such as perceived closeness, opportunities for self-expression, shared confidences, and mutual helping (clearly elements of emotional support) that are much more influential in affecting the process of adaptation than the quantitative aspects.

The results indicated that, in general, women have and use more of their social support network than men in almost every area. Women reported more often than men that they had a greater number of people in their network, obtained more practical help, had more frequent contacts, had a higher level of positive feelings for the primary members of their network, and were able to confide more deeply in the people supporting them. Gass (1989) has pointed out that one of the ways in which social support can be most helpful to bereaved adults (especially widows) is in providing them with instrumental assistance. This includes such practical necessities as learning how to drive a car, make repairs around the house, learn new occupational skills, handle legal problems, manage financial concerns, and others. Women frequently must assume these as new responsibilities after the death of a spouse if the spouse had been handling these activities while alive. The network providing supports for the females in the above areas, therefore, becomes very important to her, especially during the first year. One might speculate that the reason for the greater degree of practical help received by female survivors may lie in our social assumptions and expectations. Although the assumption may be incorrect, there is strong likelihood that the female and not the male survivor is more likely to need practical help and that he might resent or be insulted by the offer of such help.

The one area in which women did not report receiving more help than men from their supportive network was in the amount of emotional help received. Apparently, despite having fewer people to turn to for support, having less contact and not confiding so deeply as women, the men were, in general, able to find as much help for their depression and emotional distress as the women did through the resources available. It appears that, at least in terms of quality, the men were able to find much needed help in this important area of their mourning, despite the lesser amount of support.

The results also indicate that the social supports fluctuated over the 2 year period. In general, the 6-month point seemed to be most difficult, with less practical and emotional help received, accompanied by less confiding in their supportive networks. It may be, as Parkes (1985) has suggested, that 6 months is a point in their mourning at which the full impact of the loss has sunk in and the grief and sadness are most fully realized, without the opportunity as yet to fill the void and to restructure their lives.

There were also notable differences for group and for gender within each group over the course of the 2 year bereavement period. The survivors of natural deaths reported keeping roughly the same level of feelings for the people in their network over the entire period, while the suicide survivors, especially the males, fluctuated considerably over the 2 years. For both groups of grieving survivors, the most important persons in their network were family members, most often children, followed by close friends, and then siblings. In their study of rural bereaved elders, Van Zandt, Mou, and Abbott (1989) found that family was most helpful at all times, from immediately after death to $3\frac{1}{2}$ years post-death. One interesting difference from our results was that they also found that the church was helpful in the early bereavement stages, while our study found use of the church to be minimal at all times. This may well be related to rural/urban differences in the two populations studied. Both populations reported increased use of friends in the later stages of bereavement.

The 6-month low spot in social supports for the natural death survivors was primarily in practical help received, while for the suicide death survivors it centered on emotional support obtained. However, both the practical and emotional supports increased by the end of the first and into the second year, with final levels generally rated as the same or higher than immediately after death. Gender differences within the two bereaved groups appeared over the 2-year period for emotional support. Both male and female survivors of natural deaths reported receiving the least amount of emotional help at 6 months, but got more by the end of 1 year and also at 2 years. Among the suicide survivors, in contrast, the females and males reported getting practically the same level of emotional help throughout the entire 2-year period. Females among the natural death survivors showed some fluctuation in the first year in the level of their feelings toward the people in their support network, but ended at the same level by the end of the second year. Males, on the other hand, after fluctuation in the first year, showed some increase in the level of feelings toward the persons in their support network by the end of the second year.

In summary, the major findings of this study indicate that the period in time after death which seems to be most difficult for bereaved spouses of both elderly suicide and natural deaths is around 6 months, when emotional distress is high, grief and depression are still marked, support networks are used least often, and loneliness and loss are felt most intensely. Social networks play a more significant role for women in terms of obtaining more practical help, feeling more positively about them, and confiding in them more deeply than the males. Most importantly, natural death survivors get more emotional support from their network than survivors of suicide deaths, with the latter receiving even less than persons who have not suffered the loss of their spouse by death over the last 5 years. The low spot at 6 months for the natural death survivors is felt especially in the amount of practical help received; for the suicide death survivors it is primarily in the amount of emotional help obtained. Males find as much help for their feelings of sadness and loss as females, despite having fewer persons in their support system, making fewer contacts, having a lower level of positive feelings for the persons in their network, and not confiding so deeply as females. Members of the family, especially children, are the most common source of support, followed by friends, then siblings.

Taken together, these results indicate that the nature of the social support network changes over time for elders according to whether the spouse's death was due to natural causes or was self-induced and according to the gender of the survivor. Overall, suicide survivors experience less social support (in a quantitative sense), particularly on the dimensions of extent of emotional and practical support received, and particularly at the T_2 measurement point (about 6 months after their spouse's death). The suicide survivors also did not feel they could confide any more deeply in persons in their network than did the non-bereaved comparison group. This pattern of findings appears related to our previously reported findings that feelings of grief and depression take longer to subside in the suicidally bereaved. It may be that grief and depression remain intense for this group because of the relative insufficiencies that were found in the social support network of the suicide survivors. The general pattern of results also supports the contention that there are gender differences in social support, with women reporting they receive more support overall than men. This may be related to prior research (see Osterweis, Solomon, & Green, 1984) that bereaved women tend to complain more and thus ask for help to a greater extent than do widowers, who typically either develop health problems or die within 2 years of the death of their spouse, but do not generally seek help for the pain of their loss.

It should be noted that there are limitations to the generalizability of findings from this study. The subjects were volunteer participants who were generally of a middle-class socioeconomic background and who agreed to participate in a longitudinal research project. Also, we do not know the extent to which these findings would be true for minority groups or for older adults coming from less advantaged or highly advantaged backgrounds. Further research is needed to address these issues. Research into the first 6 months to determine when and what changes occur leading to the decided drop in feelings or social support at that point in the bereavement process now seems highly desirable. We need also to determine how the social networks change over a longer period than the 2 years following a spouse's death. It may be that the nature of social support changes over time as a new identity is developed, as suggested by Raphael (1983). Longer term follow-ups are needed to address this issue empirically.

References

Antonovsky, A. (1979). *Health, stress and coping.* San Francisco: Jossey Bass.

Averill, J. (1968). Grief: Its nature and significance. *Psychological Bulletin, 70,* 721–748.

Bankoff, E. A. (1983). Social support and adaptation to widowhood. *Journal of Marriage and the Family, 45,* 827–839.

Cain, A., & Fast, I. (1966). Legacy of suicide. *Psychiatry, 29,* 406–411.

Dimond, M. F., Lund, D. A., & Caserta, M. S. (1987). The role of social support in the first two years of bereavement in an elderly sample. *The Gerontologist, 27,* 599–604.

Farberow, N. L., Gallagher, D. E., Gilewski, M. J., & Thompson, L. W. (1987). An examination of the early impact of bereavement in psychological distress in survivors of suicide. *The Gerontologist, 27,* 592–598.

Farberow, N. L., Gallagher, D. E., Gilewski, M. J., & Thompson, L. W. (1991). Long term mental health/grief/personality changes in the bereavement of survivor spouses of elderly suicides. Manuscript submitted for publication.

Gallagher, D. E., Breckenridge, J. N., Thompson, L. W., & Peterson, J. A. (1983). Effects of bereavement on indicators of mental health in elderly widows and widowers. *Journal of Gerontology, 38,* 565–571.

Gass, K. A. (1989). Health of older widowers: Role of appraisal coping, resources, and type of spouses death. In D. A. Lund (Ed.), *Older bereaved spouses* (pp. 79–94). New York: Hemisphere Publishing Co.

Gilewski, M. J., Farberow, N. L., Gallagher, D. E., & Thompson, L. W. (1991). Interaction of depression and bereavement on mental health in the elderly. *Psychology and Aging, 6,* 67–75.

Glick, I. O., Parkes, C. M., & Weiss, R. (1975). *The first year of bereavement.* New York: Basic Books.

Heyman, D. K., & Gianturco, D. T. (1973). Long-term adaptation by the elderly to bereavement. *Journal of Gerontology, 28,* 359–362.

Holmes, T. H., & Rahe, R. H. (1967). The social adjustment rating scale. *Journal of Psychosomatic Research, 11,* 213–218.

Lopata, H. K. (1973). *Widowhood in an American city.* Cambridge, MA: Schenckmen.

Lund, D. A. (Ed.) (1989). *Older bereaved spouses: Research with practical applications.* New York: Hemisphere.

Lund, D. A. (1989). Conclusions about bereavement in later life and implications for interventions and future research. In D. A. Lund (Ed.), *Older bereaved spouses* (pp. 217–231). New York: Hemisphere.

Lund, D. A., Caserta, M. S., & Dimond, M. F. (1986). Gender differences through two years of bereavement among the elderly. *The Gerontologist, 26,* 314–320.

Osterweis, M., Solomon, F., & Green, M. (1984). *Bereavement: Reaction, consequences and care.* Washington: National Academy Press.

Parkes, C. M. (1985). Bereavement. *British Journal of Psychiatry, 146,* 11–17.

Raphael, B. (1983). *The anatomy of bereavement.* New York: Basic Books.

Saunders, J. M. (1981). The process of bereavement and resolution: Uncoupled identity. *Western Journal of Nursing Research, 3,* 319–332.

Schuchter, S. R., & Zisook, S. (1986). Treatment of spousal bereavement: A multidimensional approach. *Psychiatric Annals, 16,* 295–305.

Van Zandt, S., Mou, R., & Abbott, D. (1989). Mental and physical health of rural bereaved and non-bereaved elders: A longitudinal study. In D. A. Lund (Ed.), *Older bereaved spouses* (pp. 25–36). New York: Hemisphere.

9

Rational Suicide Among the Elderly

Derek Humphry
National Hemlock Society

ABSTRACT: Old age, in and of itself, should never need to be a cause for self-destruction. But suicide and assisted suicide carried out in the face of terminal illness causing unbearable suffering should be ethically and legally acceptable. This paper outlines a perspective on rational suicide—the final exit—among the elderly.

Not long ago I was invited to speak on the subject of voluntary euthanasia to a senior citizens' club in Los Angeles. As I walked into the club headquarters in the basement of a high-rise building, I wondered why they had asked me. I soon found out when the clergyman who was chairing the meeting said: "We've asked the head of the Hemlock Society to come and talk to us because, as you all know, we've lost two members recently who jumped from the roof."

Although an avid follower of local news, I had not heard about this. Apparently the two deaths had gone unreported. Suicide in Los Angeles obviously cannot compete with the city's other momentous events.

Momentarily, this cause for my presence threw me off guard. The Hemlock Society does not advocate suicide per se: It believes suicide and assisted suicide carried out in the face of terminal illness causing unbearable suffering should be ethically and legally acceptable.

Old age, in and of itself, should never be a cause for self-destruction. But whether we like it or not, the effects of aging are, for some people, sufficient cause to give up. I have come to realize that a great many of the Hemlock Society's 40,000 members believe that the organization does not go far enough in its objectives: They tolerate our limited aims but would prefer that we also fought for the right of the elderly to choose a dignified and assisted exit.

Some of these people are my friends and acquaintances, and it is fatuous for psychologists and psychiatrists to claim, as most do, that they are temporarily mentally ill or depressed. These are solid, thinking, planning people. They could be your parents!

Some of the elderly people I have met since I became executive director of the Hemlock Society in 1980 have taken their lives. In a few cases I knew them right up to within days of their suicide and saw nothing exceptional about the daily conduct of their lives. In fact, it may be the case that the more lucid and rational the person, the more likely the suicide, for they can assess the balance-sheet of their situation more coolly.

I recall the various after-effects of the suicide of one Hemlock member I knew who, at 85 and widowed the previous year, took an overdose and died. There was no terminal illness, but her horror of having a stroke and spending her final years in the hospital was unbearable now that her beloved husband was gone and her children grown and scattered. She could see no point in going on and risking a prolonged dying.

Two days later the man who rented the upper part of her house called in great distress. "She was such a lovely person," he wailed. "Why did she do it? Why didn't she tell us? I saw her walking in the garden the previous evening and she seemed her usual self."

I told him that I too admired the intelligence and poise of this woman. I reminded him that she had been a regular attender of Hemlock conferences for years and had clearly thought the matter through very thoroughly. "She was entitled to the privacy of her own decision-making," I added. We chatted for a while and he felt better.

Two years later when I was addressing a public meeting in Honolulu, Hawaii, a young man in the audience asked my view on elder suicide. Afterwards, he came up to me and said that he was the grandson of this woman. Then, in 1990, a woman approached me at the end of a meeting in Dallas, Texas, and introduced herself as her daughter. Both told me that they had come to the Hemlock meeting to hear more about the organization to which their relative had belonged, and that it was cathartic for them to share the experience. They were still coming to terms with the manner of the death.

Sometimes I hear of elderly people who, on seeing the early signs of a break-down in physical health, or what they think is the onset of senility, proceed to end their lives by overdose. Quietly, unceremoniously, with tremendous care not to inconvenience or shock others, they will self-destruct. Their fear of losing control and choice is so great that they will willingly shorten their lives.

And I am saddened. We may have lost a valuable life too soon. I believe that if we were able to offer them the option of lawful medical euthanasia they would in most cases hang on to life for a bit longer. If they could make a firm deal with their physician that he or she would provide the means for a certain exit at the point of serious deterioration, they would clutch at it.

The prospect of euthanasia can extend, not shorten, life.

In the Netherlands, as well as physician aid-in-dying for the terminally ill, there is also lawful assisted suicide for the elderly. It is not a procedure which the Dutch take lightly. The decision of the doctor to help is arrived at—if it is appropriate—after time and reflection by everyone concerned. The family is closely involved with the consideration of the request to die.

Those most likely to get medical help to die are (a) elderly, (b) in poor health, (c) making a persistent and consistent request for help with death. It doesn't happen extensively—in fact, no more than 4% of all deaths in the Netherlands are attributed to euthanasia.

It is the consolation of euthanasia's availability that is the boon to Dutch senior citizens, and a benefit as well for the rest of the public, which is spared the prospect of bodies mangled by guns and jumping.

Besides avoiding violence, the Dutch seniors do not need to end their lives in a lonely and covert manner. Because it is lawful and acceptable to be helped to die, the family is usually present or nearby when the doctor administers the lethal dose. Many, many American seniors tell me that they dearly wish such an option was available to them.

They believe that it is a basic civil liberty to be able to end their lives at a point they choose. They are offended by the thought of having to make their exit in a secretive and ultimately violent manner.

While the Hemlock Society's principal mission is to achieve physicians aid-in-dying (through assisted suicide or direct euthanasia) for the terminally ill, there is huge pressure amongst our membership to go one step further and obtain this service for the ailing elder. The very fact that there is an entire book devoted to the subject—not to mention numerous other articles—authenticates their concern.

Our critics will call it the "slippery slope," but I predict that after the problems of helping the terminally ill are solved, the question of aid to the elderly in dying will, by sheer force of public opinion, have to be addressed ethically and legally. Ex-Governor Richard Lamm of Colorado, who made a shattering speech about the rationing of health care costs in the 1980s, suggesting that the elderly were taking more than their fair share, now says that the elderly people were his most ardent supporters.

Let's not forget that the elderly have considerable financial and political clout. More of them take the trouble to vote than the younger section of the population.

How can it be a slippery slope if it is what a certain section of the public is democratically asking for? A slippery slope is when government moves in and insists on euthanasia for nefarious reasons. We must never allow that to happen. I do not think the older generations will let it occur—they are too independently minded!

A Hemlock member wrote me this letter which typifies, I think, a great many of the attitudes of the elderly:

Your emphasis is, of course, on deliverance from terminal illness and excessive pain, but there are two kinds of pain: physical, which we can all understand, and emotional, which one must experience to understand. It can be as fierce as the physical and probably less acceptable as it is less visual and could be taken advantage of.

I am 81-years-old, a good span of years. I have always had exceptionally good health. I had a happy marriage. I have a kind family and am financially secure. I have an attractive and convenient home and a pretty garden.

But the future is crowding me. I have lost a most beloved husband and a splendid son. The suffering doesn't diminish but in fact is augmented as my need of them increases and I grow older and more vulnerable.

I have already lost favorite neighbors and most of my close friends were in an in-between age bracket, about five years younger than my husband and about five years older than I. They are now, those left, moving into their upper eighties and dropping by the wayside.

My two sons, who are exceedingly good to me, live some distance away. They have busy lives of their own, families to care for and move in a different generation. Life will become more difficult for me and for them as I age.

I see a man I admired becoming senile; I see oldsters beset with all kinds of ailments, physical and emotional; I see a multitude in wheelchairs and in resthomes just waiting to die, all suffering from the pain of loneliness!

We really do not belong to anyone. As children we were first with our parents; first then with our spouses; later, first with our own young, but then the mate dies and the children have homes of their own, we oldsters are not first with anyone anymore. We are fifth wheels, forgetful, awkward and then a burden to someone.

In thinking about deliverance, have you ever addressed yourselves to the proposition that there are many who would like to be on their way before that troublesome, heart-breaking deterioration destroys us?

After a full life, should we not be able to choose to terminate it? So our children could remember us as a whole person, not a vegetable? A declaration of intent, then a span of time, like six months to be sure, and then a return to the hospital or clinic where this kind of thing could be set up to ask for a lethal pill or shot in the arm. Don't you think this idea has merit?

Recently a Hemlock member wrote in the newsletter, *Hemlock Quarterly,* about the suicide of her father, saying that she was happy for him. She explained her attitude this way:

How can a daughter who loves her father be happy that her father committed suicide? He was not ill; in fact he had been swimming that morning. But for my father, life was over. He was healthy, but he was 88 years old. He could still see but not well enough to sustain long periods of reading; he could hear, but the sounds of music or words from a television show were blurred; he could walk but not long enough to play golf; he loved to talk about the past but his friends were all gone. He was bored.

Suicide is a process. It creeps slowly into a person's mind and if the person expresses his feelings, those feelings engulf the whole family. My father was open with his thoughts for over a year, but we didn't listen. He was particularly concerned with the idea that he was going to become a burden to us. He was afraid of losing his independence.

This man, comfortably off, living in the warmth of Florida, still married, Jewish, put a plastic bag over his head as he lay in bed, and died.

I think society now needs to come to terms with elder suicide. The subject requires our tolerance and understanding of what it is like to be hovering at the point of a living death without the release that death brings to some. There should be regular, local, open forums held for seniors to discuss the pros and cons of their suicides. Only with honesty and frankness of a caliber not yet practiced, by all of us, will elder suicide be kept to the bare minimum.

10

A Rational Approach to Rational Suicide

Joseph Richman, PhD

ABSTRACT: Suicide is a reaction to internal and external sources of stress and the impact of life events. In the elderly these situations are prevalent in many who are not suicidal and instead choose life. They represent what may be called rational nonsuicide. They are far more frequent than rational suicide. Nevertheless, considerably more is written about rational suicide than its alternative. The reasons for this phenomenon are reviewed, and suggestions are made for a rational approach to the affirmation of life rather than its rejection, even to the very end.

I do not believe that rational suicide is an entity that is essentially different from other forms of self-inflicted death. However, in my treatment, I appeal to the rational in people are are contemplating suicide. This approach includes understanding reasons, reducing tensions, considering alternatives, and exploring in depth the circumstances that led to the individual's desire to die or decision to commit suicide. To imply that there are no cognitive errors behind rational suicide—that it is always the free choice of an individual, that there need be no contact with a counselor, no exploration of the decision, and no bringing in of the family or other support systems—is neither rational nor irrational; it reflects ignorance.

Suicide in the elderly can be understood as a reaction to stress and to various life events, almost all of which involve other people to various degrees. An examination of Table 1, which summarizes the major demographic and other characteristics associated with suicide, can serve as a check list of danger signs. The more of these danger signs, the greater the risk of suicide.

TABLE 1.   Recognition and Recovery Factors: The Most Frequent Signs

RISK FACTORS

1. Depression.
2. Paranoia or a paranoid attitude.
3. Rejection of help; a suspicious and hostile attitude towards helpers and society.
4. A major loss, such as the death of a spouse.
5. A history of major losses.
6. A recent suicide attempt.
7. A previous history of suicide attempts.
8. A major mental, physical, or neurological illness.
9. Major crises or transitions, such as retirement or imminent entry into a nursing home.
10. Major crises or changes in others, especially among family members.
11. Typical age-related blows to self-esteem, such as loss of income or loss of meaningful activities.
12. Loss of independence, when dependency is unacceptable.
13. Expressions of feeling unnecessary, useless, and devalued.
14. Increased irritability and poor judgment, especially following after a loss or some other crisis.
15. Alcoholism or increased drinking.
16. Social isolation: living along; having few friends. The social isolation of a couple is also associated with suicide.
17. Expression of the belief that one is in the way, a burden, or harmful to others.
18. Expression of the belief that one is in an insoluble and hopeless situation.
19. Communication of suicidal intent: the direct or indirect expression of suicidal ideation or impulses. Included, too, are symptomatic acts, such as giving away valued possessions, storing up medication, or buying a gun. In this area is the presence of previous suicide attempts and a family history of suicide.
20. Intractable, unremitting pain—mental or physical—that is not responding to treatment.
21. Feelings of hopelessness and helplessness in the family and social network.
22. Feelings of hopelessness in the therapist or other helpers, or a desire to be rid of the patient.
23. Expression of a belief in ageism, especially that the aged should not be.
24. Acceptance of suicide as a solution.

RECOVERY FACTORS: RESOURCES AND ABILITIES

A Capacity for:
1. Understanding.
2. Relating.
3. Benefitting from experience.
4. Benefitting from knowledge.
5. Acceptance of help.
6. Loving.
7. Wisdom.
8. A sense of humor.
9. Social interest.
10. A caring and available family.
11. A caring and available social network.
12. A caring, available, and knowledgeable professional and health network.

Nevertheless, the risk of false positives is also great, because so many elderly people are subject to the deaths of loved ones, illnesses in themselves and others, various blows to self-esteem, and all of the other conditions associated with suicide. However, few are suicidal, even among those who are terminally ill. That is because old age is not for sissies.

The identification of suicidal potential includes (a) features that apply to all ages, and (b) features that are specific to the elderly. The ones common to all ages include the four parameters that I have presented elsewhere (Richman, 1986). These parameters are (1) the exhaustion of the resources and coping abilities of the individual; (2) the exhaustion of the resources of the family and other support systems, or their unavailability; (3) the presence of a crisis or crises that appear insoluble to everyone; and (4) the acceptability of suicide as a solution.

The aspects specific to suicide in the elderly include a failure to complete the basic developmental tasks from birth to old age (Erikson, 1950), starting with the development of trust and continuing through initiative, industry, autonomy, identity, intimacy, generativity, and ego integrity. Completed successfully these stages represent an affirmation of the self, of relationships, and of life. However, conflicts arising from developmental processes do not appear only at the appointed life stage, but are revived at every developmental crisis. Problems with all the developmental tasks return in full force in the ill elderly. Failures or disruptions in these tasks, ranging from the three Ds—distrust, disgust, and despair—and including failures in all the other life tasks, lead to a disconfirmation of life, the worth of the self, and relationships with others.

Recovery from the suicidal state in the elderly is based upon relationships that support a sense of worth as an individual and provide a sense of belonging and social cohesion. The assets of the elderly, such as their increments in knowledge, understanding, wisdom, and sense of humor, are utilized in the recovery process. The recovery signs are as important an aspect of suicide prevention as the danger signs (see Table 1). They can be seen as the foundation of the "life enhancing" alternative to suicide proposed by Boldt (1987). However, they tend to be disregarded in most of the literature.

The decision to commit suicide does not arise overnight, but is part of a lengthy process during which the significance of the person's entire existence has been called into question. The life review (Butler, 1974) is a natural part of that process. Butler has made an enduring contribution to the understanding and treatment of the elderly in his presentations of the importance and value of reminiscence and the life review. One of my few disagreements with Butler concerns his statement that the elderly have no future; I believe that their future is very important.

A rational approach to life and death events by the elderly, in fact, requires a review of past experiences, the present situation, and, in addition, what is required for the future. The future combines all the unfinished and unsolved tasks, problems, and conflicts with a consideration of how to manage and resolve all of them.

The life review, in sum, encompasses past, present, and future, especially in those who are terminally ill. Such a life review provides a foundation that places the older person in a position to make genuine life and death choices. Frequently, the resolution of these unfinished tasks can best be accomplished through meetings with a professional counselor or therapist, preferably including family sessions. Opposition to such help can severely limit the possibilities for a truly free choice. In fact, "free choice" is inimical to rational suicide. I agree with Boldt that "suicide is rarely, if ever, a freely and voluntarily chosen course of action" (1987, p. 4).

Self-inflicted deaths are particularly incomprehensible among therapists who commit suicide. Bruno Bettelheim is a dramatic example, since his work as a psychoanalyst and an educator has been so influential. Many years before his suicide, I had read that he was a member of The Hemlock Society. I wrote to him, recommending that he also present alternatives to suicide for dealing with adversity. He never responded to my letter, except perhaps by his eventual self-destruction.

According to the newspaper obituaries, Dr. Bettelheim died in the midst of family conflicts and problems of adjustment to moving to another part of the country while coping with medical illness and depression. When he told a man at a party that he felt depressed, the man's response was, "Have you heard of the Hemlock Society?" This response would not have been given to a younger depressed person. I wonder, if Bettelheim had said that he had money problems, whether the man would have said, "Have you heard of the poorhouse?"

It would have been more rational for Bettelheim to have sought psychiatric help or psychotherapy that included his family. Beck and his colleagues (Beck, Rush, Shaw, & Emery, 1979) found that negative thoughts are associated with depression. Bettelheim might have assumed that his depressive thoughts and beliefs (i.e., that his situation was hopeless and beyond help) were based upon rational thinking.

In addition, there is a great publicity campaign in favor of the view that suicide is a rational response to growing old. It is true that many elderly suicidal persons have severe problems in accepting their age. However, many of them have revealed similar problems in self-acceptance throughout their lives, and many felt "old" at age 15. In my work since

1965 with over 800 suicidal persons, many of them elderly and ill and some of them terminal, I can state unequivocally that suicide is not a rational response to aging.

The situation, however, has changed since 1948 when I began my professional career. We are now at the dawning of the age of longevity, an age of medical miracles leading to what has been called "the biomedical revolution" (Veatch, 1976). Modern medicine has accomplished miracles, but with every miracle conditions are attached.

The increase in life expectancy and improvements in medical care have sometimes created more problems than they have resolved. More people are living today who would not have survived in the past, but their quantity of life may have been purchased at the cost of its quality. Numerous new medical and ethical decisions must be made, such as those concerning patients who are in a vegetative state or an irreversible coma.

Ours is also an age of impersonality and dehumanization in medicine, where machines and laboratory tests have replaced the doctor who made home visits and had a special relationship with his patients. Life and death issues were a natural part of that relationship. Today, such matters have become mechanized, and the picture of a stranger pulling the plug that maintains life has become the symbol of the New Euthanasia.

However, to pull the plug more frequently is not the answer, and the prevailing view in euthanasia circles that the biological state of an elderly individual is a sufficient reason for suicide is not tenable. From my experience, the reasons given for suicide, including those consciously believed, are not necessarily the most valid ones.

The supporters of euthanasia, therefore, must look at their preconceptions and root out the false ones. My basic criticism is that the euthanasia movement encourages the disconfirmation of life and discourages a life enhancing resolution to problems in living. There is much more to human rights of the elderly than the right to die.

Confronting life's tasks is an affirmative act. Avoiding them is a disconfirmation of life that culminates in ending life prematurely or finding someone to assist in that end. I have written elsewhere about the means taken to circumvent affirmation and about the unexamined assumptions of the euthanasia movement in previous papers (Richman, 1987, 1988), and will but summarize my views here.

The seven aspects of suicide, illness, and related events that are overlooked by supporters of euthanasia are as follows:

1. Illness, including terminal illness, is a crisis and crisis intervention methods are often called for. A crisis is defined as a situation where the usual means of coping are not effective and other methods must be found to help everyone through the resulting turmoil of thoughts

and feelings. The proponents of euthanasia seem unaware of the nature of crises in human life and development.

2. Suicidal intent is sometimes characterized by thinking that is mistaken, narrowed, and rigid—resulting in tunnel vision. An example is suicide that results from the mistaken belief that one has a terminal illness (Conwell, 1991). By "tunnel vision" is meant the belief that there are no alternatives and that suicide is the "only way." However, if there is no other alternative, then euthanasia is not based upon free choice but rather an absence of choice.

I also believe that dichotomizing suicides into those based on mental illness and those based on rational choice is based upon errors in thinking. All suicides, whether rational or otherwise, contain features in common. These include, in addition to the presence of a crisis, the confrontation with loss and separation, the role of others, and possible biological components. At the same time, every suicide is also unique and each one requires an understanding of a unique situation.

Therefore, to separate one type of suicide as healthy and others as sick is a rigid polarization that is found typically in the thinking of the most seriously suicidal and irrational persons. The sick–healthy dichotomy prevents understanding. It also inhibits the struggle to improve the social and other conditions conducive to suicide. The euthanasia movement, consequently, places itself on the side of social neglect.

3. Suicidal feelings are dominated by distress, fear, and loneliness. When crises around illness, loss, and death arise, all the unresolved problems and conflicts of the ill person also arise and may seem overwhelming. Meanwhile, the ill person feels abandoned by others while the loved ones perceive their abandonment by the dying person. Death wishes become ubiquitous. Then, the emotional pain, the interpersonal and family conflicts, and the stress of unfinished tasks are circumvented by the decision to commit suicide.

4. Impending death and related events lead to family reactions that are filled with pain and grief, with the ill person believing that he is a burden and the only cause of their distress. Thus, the failure to recognize that the relatives and other significant persons are in a crisis may lead to the decision for suicide. On the other hand, the recognition of the crisis nature of the situation may lead to methods of stress reduction other than suicide.

Suicide is a multidetermined, systems phenomenon involving biological, psychological, family and other social determinants. Tunnel vision usually selects just one of these, most often the biological, and even with a narrowed perception of what the biological entails.

Any "one cause" reason, therefore, is highly suspect. The feeling of the suicidal person of "being a burden" is not a valid reason for choosing death. Rather, it is the communication of tensions in the family that must be reduced; family problems need to be resolved.

There are various features of the family system and social network, especially difficulties in dealing with illness and death and with the mourning process in general, that facilitate "rational suicide." Unable to tolerate the stress, family members turn away and friends make themselves unavailable. The ill or dying person is then in a state of alienation and anomie. Therefore suicide appears rational to everyone.

Death is a phenomenon that may have profound repercussion upon the survivors, and, in this respect, suicide is no different from other deaths. Much of the work of self-help groups and therapy consists of helping the survivors deal with the loss and to grieve appropriately, whether the death is from suicide or other causes. But anticipatory grief and reactions to impending loss predate the death. When confronted openly and managed properly, it can help everyone through the process more appropriately than rational suicide.

Keeping the family from someone who is dying is a particularly undesirable act, since it prevents the resolution of the most basic unfinished tasks and conflicts as well as any final resolution.

I recall a symposium on euthanasia and rational suicide presented at the annual conference of the American Association of Suicidology in 1988. A physician presented the case of a man with AIDS, whom the presenter described as the most inspiring and genuine example of rational suicide he had ever seen. The patient was a young man who accepted his illness with courage, made his peace with his friends, and when his condition worsened to the point where he had nothing to look forward to, said his goodbyes and took a lethal overdose of pills.

During the discussion period, I asked how the patient's family had reacted to his illness. The doctor explained that his family was not present. He had never told them of his illness and kept them out of his "inspiring" last days.

"Was that rational?" I asked. "I don't know," replied the presenter. It sounded to me as though there was a great deal of unfinished business with his family that this man had left incomplete at the time of his death.

In contrast, there was a brief notice of another AIDS case in the obituary section of the New York Times on September 2, 1990, that stood in dramatic contrast to the case presented at the AAS (names have been deleted):

_____ of New York City died on September 1, 1990, at age 31, after a brave and courageous fight, of complications caused by AIDS. Beloved brother of _____, survived by dear friend _____ , and devoted and loving family members; parents, brothers, sisters-in-law, grandparents, as well as aunts, uncles, cousins and friends.

This death was neither rational nor irrational but provides an example of the inclusion of the loving family—rather than their exclusion—from the final illness of a young man, just when such love and acceptance was most needed.

5. Many supporters of rational suicide are guilty of ageism and other forms of bias. Their efforts subtly discourage measures toward improving the condition of those in need, instead offering death as a solution. For example, the cost of medical care is given as a valid and rational basis for suicide, often with a presentation of the younger and older generations in competition for scarce resources.

While congressmen and others were protesting that social measures for the elderly were depriving the young of food and shelter, those who benefitted from the savings and loan fiasco were draining the economy of upwards of 150 billion dollars. That would have been enough for social security for the elderly, housing for the homeless, self-help programs for the disabled, and education, welfare, and family programs for children. Most people would agree that these measures would have been preferable to lining the pockets of swindlers.

Many proponents of euthanasia and assisted suicides seem to assume that the elderly in our society are not wanted, despite voluminous evidence to the contrary. They state, for example, that society discards the elderly and the family does not want them (e.g., Portwood, 1978).

It is true that many of the elderly feel discarded and rejected when facing the prospect of admission to a nursing home and find death preferable to such a move. It is also true that many nursing homes are deficient in both physical and psychological care. That is an indictment of nursing homes and a call for their improvement. However, the euthanasia movement, while presenting an imminent admission to a nursing home as a rational ground for suicide, has done nothing to improve the conditions of these homes.

The research evidence does not support the views, of Portwood and others, that the elderly are not wanted. Studies in the United States clearly reveal that the majority of the aged maintain contact with their families, including those elderly who are living alone, and that they are accepted, loved, and wanted (Shanas, 1979).

6. We do not know what dark forces we may be unleashing in our society by singling out one group as worthy of death. Youth learns the acceptable norms of how to treat people of all ages from the prevailing social norms and attitudes.

Boldt (1987) discussed the possibility that the changing meanings attributed to suicide in our culture is related to the increase in youth suicide rates. In his own research (Boldt, 1982), he compared attitudes toward suicide of high school students and their parents. He found that the teen agers consistently differed from their parents, in a pro-suicide direction. He presented the well-founded concern that "our reconceptualization of suicide in terms of 'rationality' and 'rights' is providing a vocabulary of motives, meanings, and rationalizations that will be used by suicidal youth to neutralize inhibitions against suicide and to render suicide not only more acceptable, but more meaningful, purposeful, and appropriate" (1987, p. 6). Rational suicide for the elderly is a trap for the young.

7. The proponents of rational suicide discourage suicidal people from seeking help on the grounds that they are not mentally ill and therefore should not see a therapist. However, it has become increasingly recognized that you do not have to be crazy to see a psychiatrist or psychotherapist, any more than you have to be stupid to go to school. Like learning, therapy can take place throughout life, even at its very end. (I know a 97-year-old husband and an 84-year-old wife who had extremely successful marital therapy.) It is a pity, then, that so many elderly and terminally ill people have ended their lives without seeking help, and thus prevented a richer life for some and a better death for others.

The wish to die or to commit suicide is the communication of a problem that is perceived as insoluble except through the death of the suffering person. In that situation, I always respect the ill or dying persons autonomy and reach out to him or her. I offer what I have to offer and that is a listening ear and a willingness to understand, be empathic, and engage in a dialogue with the suffering person. I also bring in the family and social network. Personal autonomy should never be confused with isolation and the loss of social cohesion. When someone is suicidal I try to make contact rather than obsess over whether they have a right to live or die.

The stress involved in the families of ill persons has been a source of concern in the health professions. Studies of caregivers of patients with Alzheimer's disease, cancer, and other serious ailments have documented what a toll such caregiving can take. The ill person is often a burden.

What is to be done when a person is a burden? The usual recommendation is to provide counseling or other forms of stress management for the caregivers or significant others. That is a much more desirable procedure than rational suicide for the one who is ill. I have seen several terminally ill people in marital and family therapy, during which their lives became richer, more fulfilled, and more filled with love to the very end (Richman, 1981).

Illness is a biopsychosocial phenomenon. Therefore, effective treatment of the despairing suicidal individual must be comprehensive. Counseling or psychotherapy is as important a treatment modality to offer the patient as is medication, surgery, or hospitalization. The treatment process starts with crisis intervention, with the goal of reducing stress and increasing cohesion for everyone, and goes on from there.

It is as important to offer help and support to the family as to the patient. Those who leave out the family and friends and treat the patient as a purely biological entity living in a social vacuum are not practicing good medicine. Biological advances have helped immeasurably not only in maintaining health but in managing pain. Treatment must also consider emotional pain in the ill person and the pain caused in others because of their unresolved grief, depression, and difficulties in dealing with illness and death. That is why working with the family is so essential.

Treatment respects the views of the patient and family, even when it runs counter to the therapist. As in all therapy, a positive and trusting relationship is the basis of the treatment process.

An example in my current practice involves an 82-year-old woman who began treatment in family therapy after a major suicide attempt. She was no longer suicidal, but had a very dim view of aging, even though she was in good health and cognitively alert and intact.

In a recent session, her 50-year-old son, who is an artist, had the fantasy of himself at the age of 82, which consisted of his being alone in his studio, painting away actively. Later in the session, the mother said that if she became ill and dependent upon others she would want someone to "pull the plug." I asked her son his reaction. He agreed, saying that he would rather she was dead than be in the position of having to take care of and clean her.

I empathized with their views and told them about the living will and how to go about obtaining it. However, the topic did not end there. Toward the end of the session, I suggested to the son that he was still a very young man who has not had that much experience in helping someone in need of physical care. By the time he was 82 it might not seem such a distasteful or difficult task. He agreed, repeating, "Remember, I haven't had experience in such things."

As they were leaving and the son went for the car, his mother lagged behind and said to me, "I have such a feeling of well being."

As the example illustrates, the thought of "rational suicide" is heavily determined by the situation and the relationships existing at the time. When conflicts are resolved, individual choices are respected, and family and interpersonal relationships optimally cohesive, then there is an opportunity for a *truly* free choice. That has not been the case in the vast majority of reported cases.

Discussion

Although euthanasia literally means a good death, its failure to place a good death within a context of a good life leads to a one-sided and narrowed vision. Even so, I have had some positive experiences involving the concept.

I once appeared on the Morton Downey Show on television, but first had lunch with my wife at a restaurant across the street from the TV station. When I paid the bill, the cashier, who was Asian, asked what the topic of the program would be. "Euthanasia," I said. "Youth and Asia," she repeated, "I'm both."

Euthanasia needs more positive connotations like the one that occurred in this humorous interchange. It is infrequent to hear "euthanasia" associated with youthful spirits and pride in one's identity. These are affirmations of the self and of relationships, while euthanasia is too often a disconfirmation of these. That is why euthanasia has many critics like myself.

However, I am not criticizing euthanasia, but rather its misuse. Its criticism of the prolongation of dying when death would be a merciful release is commendable. Agreement between the sensible supporters and the flexible opponents of euthanasia is present in the avoidance of extraordinary medical measures. There is also a general recognition of the positive potentials of the hospice movement in controlling pain, providing a cheerful and loving atmosphere, and encouraging the presence of family members and other loved ones, including children.

But with criticism and proposed changes come responsibilities. Instead of hospitals that pull the plug more frequently, we need more participation by the home and families. We need loved ones and other involved people to be there and help the person to a truly good death. Without such a giving of oneself, what is called euthanasia can also be called a cop-out.

Hospitals and other institutions that are involved with the seriously ill and disabled must more actively extend their attention to the psychological, social, and family stresses faced by these patients. Norman Fost (1987) noted that many apparently ethical dilemmas faced by medicine are often based upon a lack of knowledge. His very sensible solution, therefore, was to bring all professions together to share the information.

My proposal is also to bring everyone together, but to include the patients, the family, and other significant persons. In addition to information and the sharing of ideas, persons will be given an opportunity to share and air emotional, interpersonal, and family factors.

However, not everyone is qualified to deal with such a complex situation. One recommendation, therefore, is to organize a team of medical and behavioral scientists who have had training in family crisis intervention and are knowledgeable about the medical and psychosocial nature of illness, disability, and dying. The team will be available to the medical and surgical departments of the hospital. Their goals will be to reduce the tensions and burdens in the patient and family, release the caring and cohesive forces, and ultimately permit a genuinely free choice. With the development of a more humanistic and holistic attitude, the future, I believe, is bright for the continuation of a good life and therefore a good death—to the very end.

References

Beck, A. T., Rush, A. J., Shaw, B. R., & Emery, G. (1979). Cognitive therapy of depression. New York: Guilford.

Boldt, M. (1982). Normative evaluations of suicide and death. Omega, 13(2), 145–157.

Boldt, M. (1987). Defining suicide implications for suicide behavior and for suicide prevention. Crisis, 8(1), 3–13.

Butler, R. N. (1974). Successful aging and the role of the life review. Journal of the American Geriatrics Society, 22, 529–535.

Conwell, Y. (1991). A failed suicide. Presented at the 24th Annual Conference of the American Association of Suicidology, April 19, 1991, Boston MA.

Erikson, E. (1950). Childhood and society. New York: Norton.

Fost, N. C. (1987). What is an "ideal ethical observer?" In Cross, R. (Ed.), The value of many voices (pp. 11–17). Denver, CO: Center for Health Ethics and Policy at the University of Colorado at Denver's Graduate School of Public Affairs.

Portwood, D. (1978). Common sense suicide. New York: Dodd-Mead.

Richman, J. (1981). Marital psychotherapy and terminal illness. In A. S. Gurman (Ed.), Questions and answers in the practice of family therapy (pp. 445–449). New York: Brunner/Mazel.

Richman, J. (1986). Family therapy with suicidal persons. New York: Springer.

Richman, J. (1987). Sanctioned assisting suicide: Impact on family relations. Issues in Law & Medicine, 3, 53–63.

Richman, J. (1988). The case against rational suicide. Suicide and Life Threatening Behavior, 18, 285–289.

Shanas, E. (1979). Social myth as hypothesis: The case of family relations of older people. The Gerontologist, 23, 504–611.

Veatch, R. M. (1976). Death, dying, and the biological revolution. New Haven, CT: Yale University Press.

11

Case Consultation: Mary Catherine

Alan L. Berman, PhD, Antoon A. Leenaars, PhD,
CPsych, John McIntosh, PhD, and Joseph Richman, PhD

ABSTRACT: A case of the attempted suicide of a 66-year-old female is presented. Comment based on the chapters in this volume is presented. Specific topics of demographics, psychiatric–psychological, object relations, the attempt, and concluding comments provide an idiographic illustration of suicidal behavior in an older adult.

Mary Catherine, a 66-year-old single white female, was referred for outpatient psychotherapy one week subsequent to her discharge from her first psychiatric inpatient hospitalization. She had cancelled a scheduled private follow-up session with her in-hospital psychiatrist, complaining that "he was not taking me seriously, not communicating with me well." At the time of interview, she had in her possession a discharge prescription for Prozac (20 mg, b.i.d.), which she had taken since her hospital admission.

Mary Catherine presented as an obese, balding woman with moderate psychomotor retardation. She had a noticeable tremor, primarily affecting her hands, but also her head and mouth, which she claimed to have had for "over 30 years," but increasingly so in the past 6 months. Her handwriting on the office intake form was nearly illegible. She was cooperative in interview and responsive to all questions, although she displayed a response hesitancy, apparently caused by her inability to recall particular words. A neurological consultation, voluntarily sought by the patient on referral from her cardiologist the day after her hospital discharge, proved "unremarkable," describing "benign essential tremors" not related to an intracranial lesion. An EEG revealed evidence of dysrhythmia. This finding and the observation of a nominal dysphasia suggested that she "may be suffering a mild encephalopathy."

Mary Catherine's hospitalization followed her first and only multi-method suicide attempt. Returning from work on a Monday afternoon feeling despondent and distressed, she first attempted to slit her wrist with a razor blade, but "couldn't follow through." She then turned on the gas in her apartment, hoping the carbon monoxide would end her misery. Not tolerating the wait, she then tried to drown herself in the bathtub. However, she was unable to complete this. She then dressed and went to retrieve the day's mail from the mailroom of her apartment building. In the mail was a package of flurazepam prescribed by her cardiologist and ordered through a drug supplier. She took the package, went to a nearby convenience store to buy a soft drink, then went to a park across the street and ingested 50 pills with her soda. After several minutes she returned to her apartment expecting to lie down on her bed to die, only to be met by the police who had been called by a neighbor who smelled gas in the building. Realizing now that she was not going to die, she told them what she had done and was brought to the hospital emergency room for treatment. In the emergency room she was treated by gastric lavage, monitored, then referred for psychiatric admission with a diagnosis of major depression.

In the ward she was given the usual array of inpatient treatments; the initial foci were her depressive symptoms (insomnia, anorexia, anhedonia, difficulty concentrating), obsessive preoccupations, and low self-esteem. Work-related issues were also targeted, because she recently had been granted a voluntary request for a demotion out of a supervisory role.

The overwhelming first impression of Mary Catherine was that of a highly anxious, obsessive, self-critical, and guilt-ridden woman. Much of these feelings were attached now to her recent suicidal behavior. She expressed having obsessed for about a year (ever since her symptoms had worsened) over how to suicide without being found or rescued. Now that she had made her attempt(s), she felt guilty that she had not written her will and that she had attempted suicide without having executed a Designated Power of Attorney or told her family, that is, that she could have made a "mess for others."

Mary Catherine spoke with much apprehension about the future, feeling overwhelmed and without hope ("It never will get any better," "It all will come crashing down," "The bottom will drop out.") She was now anxious and embarrassed about soon returning to work and often awoke early in the morning with dreams of "intruders in my apartment." A private woman, she spoke vaguely of "mistakes" and feared exposure. These concerns had led to her request for a work demotion, because she felt so uncomfortable with the greater responsibility and public role her last promotion had brought. She was convinced that she was unable to do what was expected of her, even though she admitted getting positive feedback about her work performance—as evidenced by her promotion.

The apparent triggering event for her current presenting symptoms was a diagnosed breast cancer 2 years previous and subsequent mastectomy, postsurgical radiation, and prosthesis. She stated that she felt "mutilated" and had refused to join a recommended support group to adjust to her new body image.

Mary Catherine was born the youngest child (of seven) in a Catholic family. Her father, recalled as benevolent, died of a stroke when she was 7 years old. For unknown reasons, all contact with her father's family ended after his death. Her mother, left in poverty, raised her children with an iron fist. Mary Catherine described her as a perfectionist, disciplinarian, and "scolder." Although "the baby" of the family and often idealized by her siblings, Mary Catherine felt she was a disappointment to her mother.

At the age of 11, Mary Catherine was diagnosed as having a heart murmur and was sent to bed for a year. She believed that both she and her mother grew interdependent during this time, her mother enjoying the companionship of having her baby around the house; Mary Catherine liking the attention she received. However, Mary Catherine lost a year of school and gained almost 50 pounds while at home. Also, puberty brought with it excess facial hair, a problem she shared with and for which she resented her mother.

Her adolescence was uneventful and limited in dating experiences. She felt she was not as good or as attractive as other girls and chose boys to date who were either unacceptable to or unavailable for a relationship. Her sexual needs were met through masturbation, for which she harbored considerable guilt.

Mary Catherine attended college and, upon graduation, took a teaching position in a small town. Facing "a world of temptations in a sea of taboos," her interest in a local man brought only anxiety and embarrassment. It was in order to avoid men and sex, she stated, that she decided to enter the convent. She stayed for more than 20 years.

At the age of 44, she left because of her envy of others in, and her desire for, a heterosexual relationship. Now more than 20 years later, she could describe only a few relationships with men, none of more than a few months' duration. Instead, she spent most of her relationship energy in the company of female friends and two of her sisters who lived nearby. Although she described these relationships as close and of great value to her, she stated that she had not sought them during her suicidal crisis because she "did not want to dump on them."

Comment

Mary Catherine's case, one representative of those treated at psycho-geriatric clinics, exhibits a number of factors that are associated with high risk for suicidal behavior. Her description touches upon demo-graphic–epidemiological, psychiatric–psychological, and sociobiological risk factors discussed in the various chapters of this volume, in addition to the issues of protection (Richman, this issue) and rationality (see Humphrey, this issue and Richman, this issue). Even though much of this volume focuses on completed suicide, an analysis of her nonfatal attempt benefits from such comparisons.

Demographics

With regard to her demographic profile, McIntosh (this issue) wisely warns against the "ecological fallacy," the error of thoughtlessly applying group findings (the "nomothetic net") to any one individual (the idi-ographic case). On the other hand, it would be equally undesirable to commit the opposite error of disregarding her fit or lack of fit with demographic and epidemiologic data.

Mary Catherine is 66, white, single, and never married. Females (see Canetto, this issue) and the young-old (see McIntosh, this issue) are at lower risk for completing suicide than are males and the old-old but at greater risk for nonfatal attempts. Marriage and family can provide protection from loneliness and isolation; being single and never married may suggest that relationship difficulties are important con-siderations in understanding Mary Catherine. We shall return to this theme later.

Old age itself does not appear to be a major factor in Mary Catherine's attempt. Aging itself is not central to most suicides of older people. Rather, as we shall see, it is the individual's history that is critical to understanding suicide and suicidal behaviors. Aging provides ample opportunity for personal history to build upon itself and for events to reactivate early life conflicts.

Psychiatric–Psychological Factors

Mary Catherine has a history of early object loss, that of her father when she was 7 years old. This loss led to the associated losses of her father's benevolence, his family, income, and financial security and a balance to her mother's cold, perhaps even harsh, discipline.

She carries a diagnosis of major depression and has had associated symptoms probably, from childhood. In addition, she suffers from significant medical and neurological ailments. She has Parkinson-like symptoms, evidence of cardiac dysrhythmia, and the diagnosis of a possible mild encephalopathy. Some of these symptoms go back "over 30 years." Health issues are often significant in precipitating suicidal behavior in older adults. The patient role appears to have had special meaning for Mary Catherine. At the age of 11, her confinement to bed significantly enmeshed her with her mother and, perhaps, to a role of dependency.

In the context of an available but unused support system, Mary Catherine responded to recent life crises (losses) with depressive withdrawal. A promotion at work led to her request to be demoted. It seems clear, here, that she grew uncomfortable in a role of relative dominance, preferring not to be in a parental and more exposed position. And although she chose her demotion, it was evidence (to her) of her incompetence and a serious blow to her self-esteem. Moreover, it harked back to her mother's critical perfectionism, becoming evidence that she was not good enough and not deserving of another's love.

Her history of breast cancer, subsequent mastectomy, and feelings of being "mutilated," combined with her history of heart murmur, her weight gain at puberty, and excessive facial hair all worked synergistically to contribute to and reinforce a long-standing poor self-image and a loss of self-worth as a woman. In turn, they fed an avoidance of available supports and, in particular, her distancing from men.

Object Relations

Mary Catherine had problems in establishing and maintaining heterosexual relationships. None lasted for more than a few months. This was a source of discontent and distress for her, as it is for many older adults (see Leenaars, this issue). Her long-standing desire for a heterosexual relationship left her unfulfilled and frustrated. It is probable that the early loss of her father was prototypic of what she came to fear in relating to each and every man. In contrast, her year in bed at the care of her mother was prototypic of her relative comfort in a protected, dependent, and female world. Her parents thus unwittingly provided motivating force for her choice of the convent. But even her attachment to the convent ended after 20 years. In her 60s, we find Mary Catherine isolated. But even more importantly, she is lonely and

living alone. Loneliness and living alone are components of social isolation that is yet another factor of risk in her case.

Although she reports a network of female friends and two sisters
living nearby, potential sources of social and emotional support (see
Richman, this issue, on recovery factors), she chose not to burden them
at the time of her suicide attempt. It is as if she is fixated in the early
stages of puberty, troubled by the emergence of a difficult womanhood,
and ill-prepared to trade her parents in exchange for her peers. Lacking
relationship to either, the damp drizzly November of her soul becomes
obvious.

The Attempt

It is a positive sign that this was Mary Catherine's first suicide
attempt. She has no lifelong suicidal career. Patients who are first
attempters later in life and who enter treatment are generally acute
and do well in treatment compared to those with more chronic histories.
(Other recovery factors [see Richman, this issue] should be noted here
as well, for example, that in spite of her history of symptoms, there is
no chronic psychiatric disability and no prior hospitalization. Furthermore, there are signs of prior competence, having graduated college
and worked throughout her life.)

The suicide methods chosen by Mary Catherine are those more often
associated with nonfatal attempts than with completions, since they
are of lower lethality than, for example, firearms or hanging. On the
other hand, the use of multiple methods of suicide is often associated
with both higher intent to die and higher lethality. Four separate
methods are noted (cutting, inhalation of gas, drowning, and ingestion
of pills), suggesting a greater intent. Compared to younger suicides,
this greater intent is a common aspect of elderly suicide (see Leenaars,
this issue). Concurrently, her behavior consistently suggests her ambivalence about dying. The case describes her not being able "to follow
through," being "unable to complete," and, ultimately, when confronted
by the police, immediately divulging her behavior and effecting her
own intervention. Thus her lethal behavior appears to have been tem-
pered by some otherwise unexpressed desire to sustain.

Her attempt in all likelihood was multidetermined. We have described
above several social and intrapsychic correlates. Might there yet be
others: monetary, biological, gender-related? Perhaps, with advancing
age, Mary Catherine has begun to anticipate economic concerns common
to the elderly (see Lester and Yang, this issue). Has she prepared for
retirement? Has her surgery raised to consciousness the possibility of

a career ending in disability? Perhaps her diagnosed mild encephalopathy is of relevance. With a diagnosed neurological problem impairing her ability to write, her request for a demotion to a less exposed or less demanding position makes sense. Moreover, it may have weakened her ego and decreased her controls against suicidal acting out. What studies were done in the hospital to document MAO activity, serotonin and/ or CSF 5-HIAA levels (see Rifai et al., this issue). Perhaps the well-documented difference between males and females regarding socialization ultimately played a crucial difference in keeping her alive. In the end, she readily accepted help. Upon discharge from the hospital she is in complaint about her inpatient therapist's empathic position and communication style, concerns common to women. But we must be cautious with these generalizations. Risk and recovery factors apply equally to males and females. A woman who gives evidence of being at risk for suicide is as much at risk as is a man with the same evaluation. We must avoid the "gender fallacy," the belief that any individual woman is less of a risk because she is a woman.

How much better is it that Mary Catherine survived her suicide attempt? Her survival first presents the opportunity to further evaluate her in a succession of diagnostic and therapeutic interviews. That she arranged and kept her outpatient interview are positive signs. That she was cooperative and communicative again are positive. If she continued to form a positive transferential relationship, that would still be more positive (see Osgood, this issue).

Other recovery factors may yet be discerned and evaluated, but the prognosis for a successful intervention in Mary Catherine's case appears quite good. This, of course, is dependent upon a formulated treatment plan, an orientation toward the identification of target symptoms, and both short- and long-range treatment goals, as well as her involvement with a competent caregiver.

Mary Catherine needs support and psychotherapy. Family sessions are warranted, particularly with her two sisters living nearby. They could discuss with her the effect upon them of being almost-survivors (see Farberow et al., this issue). If they tell Mary Catherine how much they care, the results can be very positive, not only in preventing suicide, but in increasing cohesion and decreasing depression. Therapy for her depression, perhaps in the form of cognitive as well as biological treatments (see Rifai et al., this issue) can be highly effective in lessening or alleviating depressive symptoms and concurrent suicidal ideation. Furthermore, support groups are available, particularly ones for post-mastectomy patients. This type of support would seem crucial to her adjustment to a new sense of herself *and* in decreasing her social isolation and accompanying depressogenic cognitions.

Mary Catherine expressed a desire not to be a burden on others, a theme commonly expressed by the elderly and used to promote the idea of a rational and acceptable suicide. Humphrey (this issue) illustrated his arguments with the example of an 85-year-old widow who missed her husband; her children were grown and scattered. Like Mary Catherine, we believe that this widow had a number of therapeutic alternatives, including finding a widow and widower's group. There can be life after the death of a loved one. As one elderly widow said, when asked how she could live such an active social life after her husband died, "He's dead, not me."

Both these case examples describe the need to deal with bereavement. Mary Catherine perhaps has yet to mourn her late childhood, in addition to a partial loss of her physical self. There is unfinished business that both life and psychotherapy provide the opportunity to deal with.

She is not terminally ill and she has a psychiatric diagnosis. Thus Humphrey's arguments do not apply to her case. Her decision to attempt to end her life was based on conditions of psychic pain (a response to loss), apprehension about the future, feelings of being overwhelmed, shame, and feared exposure. These are all fodder for the therapeutic mill, not causes for rational decision making.

There is no evidence presented to document an imminent decline, nor reason to believe she has no hope for many productive and potentially satisfying years ahead. Mary Catherine has ample opportunity for a decision for life. She already has declared some allegiance to the idea of continuance. She is likable, bright, emotionally accessible, intelligent, and well-motivated. Put simply, she remains a most viable human being. Her case reflects well Kastenbaum's words (this issue) that society (and policy makers) has an obligation to create a milieu that supports her viability. We hope that the papers in this volume sufficiently enrich our understanding of this population to better meet their needs and provide resources and treatments effective at helping our elders continue to enrich us all.

12

Other Books on Suicide and the Older Adult

John L. McIntosh, PhD, Antoon A. Leenaars, PhD,
C Psych, and Joseph Richman, PhD

Below is a list of books that have thus far been published on the topic of suicide in older adults. Also listed are the three books that have included in their titles the concept of "life-span" aspects of suicide. As can be seen, it is a short and largely recent list that helps to illustrate the need to further investigate and understand suicidal behavior among this group. The brief descriptions that follow are not intended to be book reviews or to be evaluative, but rather to inform the reader about the content and focus of each book.

Suicide over the Life Cycle: Risk Factors, Assessment, and Treatment of Suicidal Patients. Susan J. Blumenthal and David J. Kupfer (Eds.). (1990). Washington, D.C.: American Psychiatric Press (ISBN 0-88048-307-5) 799 pages.

This large volume consists of 27 chapters divided into three sections and a synopsis/epilogue. These sections present the epidemiology of and risk factors for suicide (biochemical, genetic, and environmental factors, as well as psychopathology, personality, substance abuse, and physical illness), assessment and management strategies (with chapters for specific age groups and other chapters on psychotherapy, cognitive approaches, and community strategies), and a number of special issues (suicide clusters and media, international issues, minorities, physician suicide, surviving the suicide of a client, ethics, and youth suicide's implications for policy and research).

Depression and Suicide in Late Life. Diego De Leo and Rene Diekstra (Eds.). (1990). Bern: Hogrefe & Huber Publishers (ISBN 0-920887-66X) 272 pages.

This 14-chapter edited volume attempts to provide an explanation of the greater prevalence of depression and suicide in the elderly. The first part of the book presents general issues (epidemiology, characteristics of depression, psychosocial factors, neurochemistry, alterations of cerebral blood flow, as well as specific attention to Parkinson's disease and mania). The book also outlines treatment and prognosis issues (e.g., pharmacology, benzodiazepine therapy, psychological issues) and concludes with a chapter about late life and preventive strategies.

Final Exit: The Practicalities of Self-Deliverance and Assisted Suicide for the Dying. Derek Humphry (1991). Secaucus, NJ: Carol Publishing (ISBN 0-9606030-3-4). (Originally published and distributed by the Hemlock Society.)

In August of 1991, this book reached the top of the *New York Times* bestseller list for advice books. The author makes arguments for the ready availability of suicide for the terminally ill. Included in this controversial book is precise information regarding methods of suicide. For a sample of the arguments and content of the book, see Mr. Humphry's chapter in this volume. The issue of assisted suicide is an important one for the elderly as a group, but Humphry's book is targeted for the larger group of terminally ill individuals.

Prescription: Medicide-The Goodness of Planned Death. Jack Kevorkian (1991). Buffalo, NY: Prometheus Books (ISBN 0-87975-677-2). 268 pages.

This book was being published and released at the time the present volume went to press. The book reportedly outlines Kevorkian's arguments for physician-assisted suicide, which he prefers to rename "medicide." The publication of this book follows the controversial and highly publicized 1990 case of Janet Atkins, a 59-year-old in the early stages of Alzheimer's Disease who committed suicide utilizing a machine built by Dr. Kevorkian. Ultimately, charges against Kevorkian were not brought to trial.

Life-Span Perspectives of Suicide: Time-Lines in the Suicide Process.
Antoon A. Leenaars (Ed.). (1991). New York: Plenum (ISBN 0-306-43620-5) 325 pages

This 20-chapter edited volume provides a perspective on suicide within the framework of development across a lifetime rather than simply focusing on one life period. Multiple theoretical perspectives are followed by chapters on epidemiology, specific life periods, correlates of suicide (biological, social, cross-cultural), issues of survivors of suicide in young people and adults, as well as prevention of suicide at different points in the time-line of the human lifespan. The book concludes with a conceptualization that, though suicide is in many ways the same across the entire life span, understanding the time lines (including those of the elderly) in the suicide process is imperative.

Suicide after Sixty: The Final Alternative. Marv Miller. (1979). New York: Springer (Vol. 2 of the Springer Series on Death and Suicide; ISBN 0-8261-2780-0) 118 pages

This was the first professional book on elderly suicide. Miller's slim book reviews the empirical literature on elderly suicide up to the mid- to late- 1970s, with particular attention to the specific factors associated with suicide among older adults (e.g., physical illness, mental illness, retirement, death of spouse, etc.). The book concludes with a detailed case of an elderly suicide (although cases are utilized throughout the book) and suggestions regarding prevention of suicide in older adulthood.

Suicide in Older Adults: Selected Readings. Sharon Moore and Bryan Tanney. (Eds.). (1991). Calgary: SIEC (ISBN 0-9691846-1-1) 89 pages

This small volume consists of six chapters providing the reader with reprinted articles. Major themes include epidemiology, suicide in institutions, characteristics of suicidal behavior, treatment, and ethics. The volume concludes with a list of recommended readings.

Suicide in the Elderly: A Practitioner's Guide to Diagnosis and Mental Health Intervention. Nancy J. Osgood (1985). Rockville, MD: Aspen (ISBN 0-87189-088-7) 240 pages

Osgood (with two chapters contributed by other authors) first provides coverage of "at-risk" older adults, followed by general overview chapters on depression assessment, etiology, and the assessment of well-being in the old (life satisfaction, morale, stress, loneliness; several published instruments are included). A chapter on the assessment of suicidal risk in the old concludes the first part of the book on diagnosis and assessment. The second part discusses (in seven chapters) specific intervention strategies to lessen suicidal risk in older adults (e.g., practitioners and their role, pharmacology, support groups, life review therapy, creative therapies).

Suicide Among the Elderly in Long-Term Care Facilities. Nancy J. Osgood, Barbara A. Brant, and Aaron Lipman. (1991). Westport, CT: Greenwood Press (Contributions to the Study of Aging, Number 19; ISBN 0-313-26522-4) 199 pages

This book outlines (in Part II) a national survey of nursing home administrators in an initial attempt to determine the extent to which suicidal behavior (direct and indirect; fatal and nonfatal) occurs in nursing home and other elderly institutional residents. Part I of the book provides an overview of long-term care settings and the approach of the environmental or social-ecological viewpoint in these settings. After Part II's study details, Part III reviews late-life depression (found prevalently in the suicidal elderly in the study) and its treatment. The book concludes with suggestions about changes in long-term-care institutional settings that might prevent elderly suicide and a chapter on the ethical dilemmas and legal aspects of elderly suicide in institutions.

Suicide and the Elderly: An Annotated Bibliography and Review. Nancy J. Osgood and John L. McIntosh (1986). Westport, CT: Greenwood Press (Bibliographies and Indexes in Gerontology, Number 3; ISBN 0-313-24786-2) 193 pages

This book provides a number of components to the question "What is known about elderly suicide?" Following a brief overview of the demographic aspects, theoretical explanations, assessment and prevention, ethics, and future areas of study with respect to suicide among older adults, the book's major bulk is comprised of annotated bibliographic citations of the literature on elderly suicide written in English and covering the time period up to 1985. Separate chapters are included for other bibliographic sources, reviews, and other nonempirical works (the 84 annotations in this chapter include sections on case studies and ethics); empirical investigations (113 works are annotated); and a listing of non-English-language works.

Common Sense Suicide: The Final Right. Doris Portwood. (1978). New York: Dodd, Mead (ISBN 0-396-07536-3) 142 pages. This book is currently available from the Hemlock Society.

The author discusses and argues for the right to suicide among older adults in the absence of legalized euthanasia. Among the arguments presented is that the old are able to assess the positive and negative aspects of life, and if the negative outweighs the positive on a "balance sheet," then the older adult should have the right to commit suicide. Portwood discusses the plight of the elderly in modern society, as well as legal and religious issues of elderly suicide, in which she concludes that suicide should be neither a crime nor a sin. Possible benefits to the individual and others and the practical aspects of what might be done if and when suicide for the old is legalized are presented.

The Last Choice: Preemptive Suicide in Advanced Age. C. G. Prado. (1990). Westport, CT: Greenwood Press (Contributions in Philosophy, Number 14; ISBN 0-313-27301-4) 215 pages

This book presents the philosophical arguments for "preemptive suicide." Prado does *not* argue for "surcease" suicide, which is suicide to stop or avoid present stressors or pain (which is what the authors Portwood, Humphry, and Kevorkian, noted above, advocate). Rather, Prado painstakingly provides arguments for a type of suicide which is "the rational way of avoiding not actual, intolerable conditions, but foreseen demeaning decline" (p. 1). The main objective of the book is to permit the consideration of suicide to be an "elective choice" rather than a "drastic response." Such suicide requires acceptance of the concept of "rational suicide," and Prado goes to great length to define and defend the concept of rationality and specifically rational suicide.

Overcoming Elderly Suicide. Joseph Richman. (1992). New York: Springer 250 pages

This is the first professional book on treatment, primarily psychotherapy, for suicidal and despairing older adults. It is written for the elderly who want help in transcending their self-destructive urges, rather than in hastening to their final exit. In 10 chapters, Richman provides the theoretical, research, and clinical background for a comprehensive and life-offering approach. In addition to a number of introductory chapters, specific chapters discuss the recognition signs, assessment interview, crisis intervention, principles of a healing relationship, and psychotherapy (individual, group, and family).

Suicide Across the Life Span—Premature Exits. Judith M. Stillion, Eugene E. McDowell, and Jacque H. May. (1989). New York: Hemisphere (Series in Death Education, Aging, and Health Care; ISBN 0-89116-630-0) 287 pages

This book provides a basic overview of the suicidology literature and suicide in specific life periods. After a brief discussion of the history of suicide as well as statistics and definitions, an overview of the many perspectives that have been utilized to explain suicidal behavior (the theoretical perspectives include the psychoanalytic, psychosocial, behavioral, biological, sociological, humanistic, and cognitive) are presented. The following chapters include separate discussions of suicide in childhood, adolescence/young adulthood, middle adulthood, and old age. The suicide literature on prevention, intervention, and postvention are briefly presented. The book concludes with an application of the concept of life-span development to the conceptualization of suicide, such that suicide is viewed not only within single age groups but as a life-long process.

Suicide in the Elderly. Ad Kerkhof and Diego De Leo (Eds.). *Crisis 12*, 1–87.

This special issue of *Crisis*, the official journal of the International Association for Suicide Prevention, consists of 10 chapters. The early chapters outline general characteristics, psychological factors, and intervention strategies. This is followed by a presentation by reports about suicide in the elderly from India, Japan, Germany, and the Netherlands, allowing the reader to get a more international perspective. The special issue concludes with chapters about "rational" suicide and the importance of awareness of the problem to a world-wide level.

Index